WILL THE WORLD END IN
2012?

WILL THE WORLD END IN 2012?

RAYMOND C. HUNDLEY, PH.D.

THOMAS NELSON
Since 1798

NASHVILLE   DALLAS   MEXICO CITY   RIO DE JANEIRO

Published in Nashville, Tennessee, by Thomas Nelson. Thomas Nelson is a registered trademark of Thomas Nelson, Inc.

Thomas Nelson, Inc., titles may be purchased in bulk for educational, business, fund-raising, or sales promotional use. For information, please e-mail SpecialMarkets@ThomasNelson.com.

Library of Congress Cataloging-in-Publication Data

Hundley, Raymond C.
    Will the world end in 2012? / by Raymond C. Hundley.
      p. cm.
    Includes bibliographical references and index.
    ISBN 978-1-4002-0285-0 (alk. paper)
    1. End of the world. 2. Eschatology. 3. Prophecies. 4. Two thousand twelve, A.D. I. Title.
    BT877.H86 2010
    236'.9—dc22   2010001046

Printed in the United States of America

10 11 12 13 14 RRD 5 4 3 2 1

This book is dedicated to my wife, Sharyn, who has stayed with me for forty years through great times and difficult times. Without her constant encouragement and excellent editing skills, this book would not exist.

TABLE OF CONTENTS

INTRODUCTION

The year 2012 has the mark of destiny upon it.

—Lawrence E. Joseph

PREDICTIONS OF THE END OF THE WORLD HAVE CAPTURED the attention and stoked the fears of generations over the centuries. One Web site cited 149 different predictions of the apocalypse between AD 44 and 2008.[1] The predictions come from Jewish theologians, Hindu gurus, New Age enthusiasts, scientists, Edgar Cayce, David Koresh, Jehovah's Witnesses, and Christian theologians. Humanity is mesmerized by the idea that the material world could cease to exist someday, and all life on the planet could be extinguished, especially if the doomsday predictors claim that the end is near. Even Homer Simpson can be seen carrying a The End Is Near sign! *Boston Globe* editorial writer James Carroll lamented: "It used to be that apocalyptic warnings about the approaching end of time came from sign-holding religious nutcases. Now they come from hard scientists."[2] Many of us seem to have a "prediction addiction" that speaks to our deepest fears and draws us to doomsday prophecies like a moth to the flame of a candle.

People habitually turn to futuristic predictions when their present-day situation becomes unbearable or intolerable.[3] The rise and fall of interest in predictions of the end of the world appear to follow the same rise and fall of stresses, dangers, and exasperation over the actual conditions of human life. Today, perhaps as never before, humanity is faced with a barrage of problems that seem almost insurmountable and that increase alarmingly every day. Some of those stresses are: population explosion, the oil crisis, species extinction, global epidemics, nuclear weapon proliferation, dangerous climate changes that increase the number and severity of hurricanes and tsunamis, major economic disruption, global warming, depletion of the ozone layer, and the violence of continuous wars and terrorism.[4] We live in a stressful, dangerous world that could implode at any moment.

In our generation, a new wave of end-of-the-world prophecies is spreading through the Internet, television documentaries, books, and movies. For example, in his book *The Bible Code*, Michael Drosnin clearly predicted the end of the world in 2012. Drosnin's code is based primarily on the work of three Israeli mathematicians (Witztum, Rosen, and Rips) in their scholarly article "Equidistant Letter Sequences in the Book of Genesis," which appeared in *Statistical Science* in 1994.[5] By applying a computer software program first created by expert code breakers that picks out Hebrew letters like words in a crossword puzzle, Drosnin has allegedly found amazing predictions in the Hebrew Bible text that speak of World War II, the assassination of the Kennedys, Watergate, the Oklahoma City bombing, and many other events that were far in the future when the Hebrew text was written.[6] Although he "insists he does not believe in God," Drosnin does firmly believe that a numerical code embedded in the Hebrew scriptural text has been placed there by "someone" to help us see the future.[7] Drosnin believes that the Bible Code was placed in the Old Testament by aliens who landed on the shores of the Dead Sea six thousand years ago.[8]

In regard to the 2012 doomsday movement, Drosnin reported: "The year 2012 also appears with 'comet' in Deuteronomy 1:4. 'Earth annihilation' appears just above in Exodus 34:10. But, with 2012, also in the hidden text of Deuteronomy 1:4 are the words 'It will be crumbled. I will tear it to pieces.'"[9] Drosnin is convinced that the hidden code behind Deuteronomy 1:4 predicts the end of the world in 2012.

Drosnin has been criticized for the arbitrary nature of his methods. In fact, Australian mathematics professor Brendan McKay has debunked Drosnin's Bible Code by applying its software to *Moby Dick* and finding six assassinations and even the death of Drosnin himself in it![10] Even worse, two of Drosnin's 1997 predictions—a world war in 2000 or 2006, and a comet striking Earth in 2006—were obviously false.[11]

Others, like Latin American José Argüelles, take a more mystical approach. In his work *The Mayan Factor*, Argüelles fixed the date for the end of the present world order at December 21, 2012, based on the ending of the Mayan calendar and the 2012 "Harmonic Convergence,"[12] in which the sun, moon, and six planets will become aligned and cause great destruction on Earth. Argüelles and others have promoted several international conferences on the 2012 doomsday prophecies since 1987, trying to bring humanity to a position of peace, love, and harmony that could avoid harsh realities from occurring in the coming transition to a new world order in 2012.[13] Christian apocalyptic expert Mark Hitchcock sees the 2012 phenomenon as "the eschatology of the New Age movement. It's their view of how this world will end or how a new age of human consciousness begins."[14]

Brothers Terence and Dennis McKenna used a painstaking mathematical approach to calculate the 2012 doomsday predictions of the *I Ching* in their work *The Invisible Landscape: Mind, Hallucinogens, and I Ching*. Prolific author John Major Jenkins has published a series of books on the 2012 event, including *Tzolkin, Maya Cosmogenesis 2012, Galactic Alignment*, and *Pyramid of Fire*. One of the most comprehensive works on the 2012 doomsday prophecies is *Apocalypse 2012: A Scientific Investigation into Civilization's End*, by Lawrence E. Joseph. And finally, the book popularly credited with beginning the 2012 doomsday movement is Daniel Pinchbeck's *2012: The Return of the Quetzalcoatl*, published in 2006. We have even seen the publication of a rather sardonic but practical work by Synthia and Colin Andrews entitled *The Complete Idiot's Guide to 2012*, published in 2008.

An ABC News survey in 2008 asked more than 250,000 participants if they expected apocalyptic events to take place in 2012. Sixteen percent of the responders answered yes. Asked if they thought the apocalypse would come from human action or divine intervention, 67 percent responded "human action." Patrick Geryl, a former laboratory worker who lives in Belgium, told ABC News: "You have to understand, there will be nothing left. We will have to start an entire civilization from scratch."[15] Geryl quit his job after he had saved up enough money for his needs up to December 2012 and is now amassing survival supplies in preparation for the apocalypse. Interestingly, Geryl based much of his certainty about a catastrophe in 2012 on his belief that the position of the stars when Atlantis sank underwater will be exactly repeated in 2012.[16]

A young person wrote the following to a Web site dealing with the 2012 doomsday predictions:

> Let me start to say that I have extreme anxiety and panic attacks all day, panic attacks that last around 12+ hours. I am an extreme worrier. I read a lot, and the 2012 talk scares me more than anything. I am 21 years old. I am not afraid of death, I am however worried about dying too young. I will be 25 in 2012. I am also not a religious man, nor do I believe in people who tell the future and other dooms day dates. I see a lot of people talking about 2012 and how we're most likely doomed, and that scares me.[17]

Many people feel a similar sense of dread as the year 2012 approaches.

The event that recently sparked great interest in the 2012 doomsday movement was the release of Roland Emmerich's movie 2012. An extensive advertising campaign by the Sony Corporation has created growing fascination with this graphic end-of-the-world film. Sony even set up a bogus Web site called The IHC: The Institute for Human Continuity.[18] The IHC confirmed that "after more than two decades of rigorous research from the worlds [*sic*] top astronomers, mathematicians, geologists, physicists, anthropologists, engineers, futurists . . . we know in 2012 a series of cataclysmic forces will wreak havoc on our planet. The IHC has developed a number of initiatives to prepare the world for this inevitability."

One of those initiatives is the supposed construction of subterranean cities all over the world that can withstand the 2012 devastation, and the other is preparation for travel to outer space colonies for survivors of the 2012 devastation. The IHC has also set up a system to distribute lottery tickets all over the world so that "each individual [will have] an equal opportunity in 2012." I registered with their site to see what would happen, and received my "unique lottery number" certificate, which will make me "eligible" to be picked for inclusion in the subterranean cities or outer space colonizations.

The *2012* movie opens with a discovery in India that massive solar flares are beginning to affect the core of the planet. The sun erupts, sending a new kind of nuclear particle bombarding the planet and changing Earth's molten core. As Jackson Curtis (played by John Cusack) and his children leave for a vacation in Yellowstone National Park, small quakes start to open up fissures all around them. Curiously, they pass a man on the street with a sign that reads, "Repent, the end is near."

They arrive at Yellowstone and discover that the army

has set up barriers to keep people out of the area. Military men, who claim that Yellowstone Park has become unstable, escort them to "safety." They meet Charlie Frost (played by Woody Harrelson), a crazy old man who tells Curtis that Yellowstone will soon become "the world's largest active volcano." Frost offhandedly ticks off the various prophecies of the end of the world in the Hopi religion, the *I Ching*, the Mayan calendar, and the Bible. He tells Curtis that the Maya predicted an expiration date for Earth and that it is coming true. Frost claims that the world's governments know all about this and have been planning to save a select group of people from the catastrophe.

Curtis and his children return home to Curtis's estranged wife, Kate, and her boyfriend, Gordon. The scene changes, and the drastic destruction begins. Earthquakes erupt all over the world. The magnetic poles begin to shift, affecting Earth's core and also its crust. Dr. Helmsley, a government scientist, warns the U.S. president of the impending disasters, who recommends immediate evacuation.

Curtis, Kate, their two children, and Gordon begin a frantic race to outrun the disaster. They hire a plane and fly away from the destruction in California, with Gordon as the reluctant pilot. Destruction and chaos follow closely behind.

The action flashes back to Charlie Frost at Yellowstone, where he is standing near the super volcano that is about to erupt, broadcasting on his backpack-rigged radio to anyone who will listen. At one point, he says, "I can only hope that all of you have made your peace with God." The volcano erupts like an atomic bomb, and Charlie is burned alive. The ash cloud from the Yellowstone volcano begins to spread all over the U.S.

Earthquakes ravage South America. The U.S. president refuses to leave Washington on *Air Force One* and dies as naval destroyers are washed into the city by monster waves. Curtis and his family accompany a rich Russian on his large plane to China to board the ships. As they fly toward China, scenes appear of the destruction on the ground. Hawaii is covered with molten lava from erupting volcanoes. Earthquakes destroy Washington. In Italy, the Vatican crumbles under the power of earthquakes. Tsunamis produced by underwater earthquake eruptions send five-thousand-foot waves crashing down on cities and mountains. All land communications cease.

The rescue vessels are not spaceships, but seven "arks" constructed in China and financed by various nations of the world to take thousands of carefully selected people — many "selected" because of their ability to pay — to safety in the floodwaters. Dr. Helmsley complains that they are leaving thousands of people to die outside the arks who would fit on board with no problem. Anheiser, the self-seeking politician in charge, counters that taking them aboard might jeopardize their plan to start a new human civilization after the devastation is over. Helmsley finally convinces the heads of state to open the gates of the arks and let the people trapped outside come in. The camera shifts to the Himalayas, where a Buddhist monk and the temple he lives in are washed away by a gigantic tidal wave. As the ark sails off, the captain receives word that Africa has not been flooded, so they set sail for Africa to start a new civilization.

It is clear that the Curtis family is being presented as a microcosm of what is happening to all the people who are rescued. They bond together as a family and forget all their former differences. As the movie ends, a large crowd of people from all faiths, all races, and all age groups stand together, readying themselves to begin a better world.

The last frame of the movie reads, "Day 27, Month 1, Year 0001."

As my wife and I were leaving the theater, I asked an older couple if they thought what they had seen was really going to happen. They answered, "Yes, it will definitely happen someday." When I asked if they thought it would happen in 2012, they said, "No." I then asked a group of four young teenagers the same two questions. "Will what you just saw really happen someday?" All four answered, "Yes, it will."

"Will it happen in 2012?"

The teenage boy answered with a strong "No," but the three girls, with eyes wide with fear, answered, "Yes, it will."

The message of the movie appears to be that a world-wide disaster might bring all of the survivors together as one big family. Nationality, religion, age, and ethnic differences would be forgotten in the struggle to survive. Emmerich pictures a new world in which people will help one another and cooperate with each other for the common good. That kind of utopia has been dreamed of by many leaders in history, from Karl Marx to Mao Tse Tung, but it has never been realized. It would be ironic if a global disaster proved to be the only way to convince people to live together in harmony, peace, and unity.

Sadly, Emmerich's vision is probably too idealistic to become reality. In the end, most people would probably react to impending danger by trampling others under their feet if it brought them closer to rescue. Human nature does not seem to be as inherently loving, self-sacrificing, and altruistic as Emmerich would like us to believe. Christian author Mark Hitchcock said:

Horrible crises . . . can bring people closer together for a while and cause people to reflect in ways they haven't before, but it doesn't take long before man's inhumanity to man begins to surface again. Man cannot usher in his own utopia by some shift in consciousness. John Lennon sang about people living in peace, yet the Beatles could not even get along with each other.[19]

Maybe a truly apocalyptic disaster would change all that. Maybe not.

Of all the experiences the movie elicits in viewers, Dr. Helmsley's wistful statement seems to echo the most in the minds of many people who see the movie: "I thought we'd have more time." Those of us who lived through the sixties will no doubt remember Larry Norman's 1969 song "I Wish We'd All Been Ready":

> *Life was filled with guns and war,*
> *And everyone got trampled on the floor,*
> *I wish we'd all been ready*
> *Children died, the days grew cold,*
> *A piece of bread could buy a bag of gold,*
> *I wish we'd all been ready.*[20]

Being ready! Perhaps that is what all of these prophecies through the ages have been trying to say to us—be ready. But how?

How can we possibly prepare for such a devastating event?

Can we trust one another to give a helping hand to the weak and vulnerable, or should we isolate ourselves in bunkers and underground shelters with no room for outsiders?

Is there some way to avoid this calamity?

As Christian author Lloyd Hildebrand said, "If the fulfillment of certain prophetic events is imminent, as many cultures and religions believe, it is crucial for you to get prepared, at least spiritually, for everything that may lie ahead."[21]

In this work, we will be looking at the end-of-the-world predictions behind this global 2012 movement in an attempt to evaluate their validity, their scientific foundations, and their meaning for us today. Surely our faith in God will play a deciding part in how we respond to this possibility of global devastation and the end of the world. Ten basic arguments for an eminent doomsday belief have been circulating in books, movies, and on the Internet.

1. **The Mayan factor.** Mayan prophecies of the end of this age come from the abrupt ending of the Maya Long Count Calendar. The calendar gives a beginning date and an ending date for humanity's time on Earth; many Mayan experts see this as a clear prediction of the end of the world.

2. **Solar storms.** Reputable scientists have predicted massive solar storms in 2012. Many believe they could trigger a chain reaction of global disasters.

3. **CERN and the Large Hadron Collider.** Experiments currently underway with the Large Hadron Collider near Geneva risk producing black hole–like particles

that could conceivably bore through the planet and destroy it.

4. **The predictions of Nostradamus.** Followers of Nostradamus unveiled a new book of watercolors by the famous French prophet that they believe signal the end of the world on December 21, 2012.

5. **The coming reversal of the North/South magnetic poles.** The solar flares predicted for 2012 could cause a reversal of the North/South magnetic poles, causing destruction and chaos.

6. **Collision with "Planet X."** Some people are predicting that there will be a collision between Earth and Planet X in 2012 that will wreak havoc on our planet.

7. **Earth's alignment with the galactic plane.** The galactic alignment of Earth, the sun, and several planets on December 21, 2012, according to many, will produce huge gravitational influences on Earth, which may even knock the planet off its axis.

8. **Eruption of the super volcano.** Competent volcanologists have identified the threat of an eruption of the super volcano that sits under the enormous volcanic cauldron at Yellowstone National Park. Some believe that the solar storm of 2012 may cause Earth's core to heat up, causing volcanoes like the one at Yellowstone to erupt almost simultaneously.

9. **The Web Bot Project.** Two brothers have affirmed that their study of futuristic trends revealed through Internet communications indicate a major cataclysmic event in 2012.

10. **Religious predictions of the end of the world.** Finally, many world religions present horrific descriptive prophecies of the end of the world. Some even identify December 21, 2012, as the date of the coming holocaust.

I devoted a chapter to each of these predictions of coming calamity and objectively considered its case and how seriously it should be taken. Each chapter begins with a brief fictional dramatization of its theme. I am a Christian. I have been a pastor, missionary, and seminary professor. But I have also been an author, a university professor, and a conference speaker. I did not dismiss any of these predictions merely because of my Christian perspectives. I have made every attempt to let them speak for themselves and present the most compelling arguments possible for their point of view. I am thoroughly committed to understanding their focus, goals, methods, and argumentation, without passing prejudiced judgment on them.

I included the thoughts of Christian leaders along with the multitude of other sources I have quoted in this book, but I did not give them preferential treatment. I also analyzed what they had to say. My hope is that both Christians and non-Christians will find in this book a careful, well-documented, and fair analysis of the 2012 phenomenon and make their own decisions about its effect on their lives.

Then we take a look at the "be ready" question, giving some suggestions for preparing for this event if it does occur in 2012. The 2012 panic may cause many people to reassess their lives and ask the ultimate questions of life:

What will happen to me when I die?

How can I live with my fear of the end of the world?

Is there any bedrock hope that can get me through this horrible devastation?

The answers to those questions may ultimately be the most constructive result of the 2012 doomsday movement for all of us. I firmly believe there are positive, useful answers that we should all consider. Finally, I directed the epilogue specifically to Christians in an attempt to draw out some of the implications of the 2012 movement for them, encouraging them to allow the 2012 phenomenon to challenge them to a richer, stronger, and more open Christian life. I am walking a tightrope here, but I am enjoying the balancing act and believe it will be of benefit for non-Christians and Christians alike.

ONE

THE MAYAN FACTOR

On that day, dust possesses the earth,
On that day, a blight is on the face of the earth,
On that day, a cloud rises,
On that day, a mountain rises,
On that day, a strong man seizes the land,
On that day, things fall to ruin,
On that day, the tender leaf is destroyed,
On that day, the dying eyes are closed,
On that day, three signs are on the tree,
On that day, three generations hang there,
On that day, the battle flag is raised,
And they are scattered afar in the forests.

— Prophecy of the Mayan Priest Chilam Balam,
    16th century

When Manuel reached the age of fourteen, his father, Don Miguel, told him it was time he learned about his heritage as a Maya. For the first time, Manuel was allowed to read the incredible Mayan documents that had been passed down to them from generation to generation. Manuel was surprised to read that the gods had made four attempts at the creation of man. The first three failed. He was especially interested in the many calendars the Maya had produced. One calendar was for short periods of time, one for religious ceremonies, and one special calendar for long time periods.

Manuel quickly learned the Mayan numbering system, based on units of twenty and a lunar calendar. He was amazed that the Maya had set the date of creation, and he was puzzled when he realized that the Long Count Calendar had an end date as well. "Papi, what does that last date mean?"

His father looked very solemn as he answered, "Son, our ancestors were great astronomers. They studied the movement of stars and planets, especially Venus. They were so good at it that they were able to predict eclipses and weather changes. Your forefathers looked into the future and saw the end of this present age."

Manuel was impressed, but he was also worried. He had one more question. "But what is that end date on the gringo calendar?"

Don Miguel's voice quivered slightly as he replied, "It is December 21, 2012, Son."

Manuel's face wrinkled as he thought how soon that date would arrive and all he would miss doing if the world ended on that day.

The Mayan empire was one of the most amazing and most gruesome civilizations in all of human history. Although the Mayan civilization began in about 2000 BC, its "Classic Period" lasted from about AD 250 to 900. It was in the Classic Period that Mayan civilization reached its high point in writing, art, architecture, and astronomy. Their empire encompassed Honduras, Guatemala, Belize, El Salvador, and central Mexico. The Maya developed large urban centers based on agriculture. There is ample evidence that they founded small villages around their central cities where the growing of corn enabled them to nourish their families well.

Mayan expert Dr. Michael Coe observed how most of the Maya lived: "Villages made up of thatched-roof houses,

in no way very different from those in use among modern
Mayan peasants now, dotted the land."[1] They lived in highly
complex social groups centered on religious practices and
a strictly ordered societal life. Local kings, "who claimed
descendance from a different god in the Mayan pantheon,
governed the large cities. Most of the time the kings were
also shamans, or holy men, and served to open portals to the
gods via ecstatic states."[2]

The Maya practiced human sacrifice as part of their religion, often using children for the ritual in which the Mayan
priest cut open the still-alive child's chest and pulled out
the heart as a sacrifice to the gods. In fact, to celebrate the
beginning of a new year, the Maya "ripped out the heart of
a sacrificial victim . . . and started a flame with a fire drill in
his open chest cavity."[3] As one Mayan expert has explained,
"Put simply, human beings were vicariously sacrificed to the
gods as reimbursement for the gift of life."[4] They also served
to appease the planet Venus, which the Maya believed
would harm them with "violent and negative influences" if
they did not offer up bloody human sacrifices.[5]

In Mayan mythology, the sun god demanded blood to continue functioning. Like believers in most mythology-centered
religions, the Maya believed that what happens on Earth also
happens in the heavenly realm. So, blood sacrifices, especially
of the heart of the victim, were a way to feed the gods and
guarantee fertile crops and well-being for the people. Since the

Maya believed that the gods gave their own blood to humans in creation, the human sacrifice ritual signified that as the heart and blood were extracted on Earth and burned in fire, the gods were nourished with their own blood. The great mythological epic of the K'iche' Maya, known as the *Popul Vuh*, records the origins of this custom.[6] Without blood sacrifices, the gods would die, and all life on Earth would die with them.

Priests were responsible for making sure such ceremonies were celebrated on favorable days, based on the movements of the stars and planets. They believed that certain days on their calendar were sacred days and therefore apt for blood sacrifices to be made to the gods. They observed, recorded, and measured the movements of the sun, the moon, and the planet Venus to determine which days were most auspicious for their ceremonies. The Maya created a special calendar to keep track of those days, based on the movements of the planet Venus, called the *Tzolk'in*.[7]

Because of that foundational belief in their religion, they were also famous for their achievements in astronomy. They had to make sure their ceremonies corresponded to specific movements of the stars and planets and seasons of the year. So, the Maya built incredible observatories at sites like Palenque, Tikal, and Chichen Itzá, where they studied the movements of stars year after year. They made very meticulous, sophisticated calculations about the orbits of the sun and the planet Venus and other stars, seasonal changes, and eclipses of the sun and moon. Without the use of telescopes, the Maya were able to calculate the exact number of days in a year with greater precision than the Gregorian calendar we use today.[8] Christian scholar Mark Hitchcock observed, "The Maya weren't just interested in time, they were obsessed with it. They were galactic masters." It is true that the Mayan calendar scholars kept incredibly detailed records of the "cycles of the moon, the sun, and Venus. Their uncanny accuracy was not duplicated until modern times."[9]

Based on their studies in astronomy, the Maya created a calendar system that plotted the history of time starting with the beginning of the current world on August 11, 3114 BC. Using a lunar calendar system, the Maya measured time in units of twenty. Twenty *kin* (days) made a *winal* (month); 18 *winals* made a *tun* (year); 20 *tuns* made a *katun* (20 years); and 20 *katuns* made a *baktun* (400 years). To designate a specific date, they recorded it in terms of how far away from the start of creation it was. So, the Mayan "long count" calendar date 6.4.8.9.17 represents 6 baktuns, 4 katuns, 8 tuns, 9 winals, and 17 kin/days from the creation of the present world.[10]

The significance of the Mayan calendar is that it appears to predict 13 baktuns as the end time of the present world age. After dating every year from the beginning of time, the calendar abruptly ends at the close of the thirteenth baktun. Translating the Mayan calendar date into the Gregorian calendar system used today produces a date of December 21,

2012, as the end-date for the present age. That is the date on which the Great Cycle of the Long Count reaches its culmination. Mark Hitchcock concluded that "the ancient Aztec calendar corroborates the Mayan end date, also pointing to the end of the present cycle as December 21, 2012."[11]

The first claim that the end of the Mayan calendar corresponds to December 21, 2012, appeared in Robert Sharer's revision of Sylvanus Morley's book *The Ancient Maya* (1983). Since that time, numerous authors have confirmed this date as the end of the Mayan calendar cycle and therefore, the end of the world. Works like those of Michael D. Coe popularized this interpretation of the significance of the Mayan calendar for many in the 2012 doomsday movement. Coe, who is emeritus professor of anthropology and emeritus curator of the Peabody Museum of Natural History at Yale University, received Guatemala's highest honor, the Order of the Quetzal, for his excellent research in Mayan culture and writings in that country. His concepts have been crystallized in *Breaking the Maya Code*, an eye-opening DVD feature documentary produced by David Lebrun. Coe's expert knowledge of Mayan culture, architecture, and glyph-writings has qualified him as a world-renowned expert in Mayan studies.[12] His endorsement of 2012 as the end date of the world adds a great deal of academic respectability to the 2012 doomsday movement's interpretations.

Confidence in the Mayan ability to understand

astronomical realities and accurately predict future events has become a mainstay of apocalyptic projections in the last two decades. The Maya are revered by many people today as the most amazing predictors of future events in human history. Faith in their ability to pinpoint the end of the world has become a basic tenet of the 2012 doomsday movement. Almost everyone who learns of the Mayan ability to track orbits, eclipses, and minute movements of stars is astounded by their advanced technological skills in spite of their lack of modern tools. Where did they gain these abilities?

Some have suggested that they must have received this sophisticated knowledge from extraterrestrials. Others have concluded that survivors of the mystical Atlantis communicated this information to them. It is known that the Maya used hallucinogenic plants, peyote, and mushrooms to place themselves in a trance in which "they were able to travel among the stars. . . . It was during trance states that some of the advanced knowledge is claimed to have been discovered."[13] John Major Jenkins referred to these drug-induced experiences favorably as "shamanistic knowledge-gathering journeys into inner space" in which the Maya were able to understand many of the mysteries of the universe through the heightened powers of hallucinogenic drugs.[14]

Mark Hitchcock believes that "they learned it from their gods, which were not gods at all, but demonic spirits. . . . Much of the barbaric, bloodthirsty 'worship' of the Mayans, including human sacrifices, can be accounted for if we recognize that it was demonically motivated by the real power behind their gods of stone."[15]

In 1987, Mayan expert José Argüelles published his influential text *The Mayan Factor*, in which he combined Mayan documentary evidence and mystical spirituality to affirm the end-of-the-world date of 2012. Argüelles and his colleagues have promoted an international 2012 movement that combines doomsday predictions with mystical teachings about being in harmony with the universe, establishing peace among all people, and openness to cosmic states of consciousness that are trying to teach us to live in unity with one another.[16] Argüelles does not see 2012 as the total end of the world, but as the end of the present world order, which will usher in a new, improved world.

José Argüelles "was honored on March 3, 2002 as 'Valum Votan, Closer of the Cycle' atop the Pyramid of the Sun at Teotihuacán by nine Indigenous Elders who awarded him a ceremonial staff for his efforts in helping to wake humanity up to the meaning of 2012."[17] So, there are certainly some important indigenous leaders who agree with Argüelles that 2012 spells the end of the present world order and the beginning of a new one.

Two questions that arise from this assertion are: (1) How does the Maya's meticulous ability to study the movement of stars and predict eclipses and weather conditions qualify them as predictors of the future and the end of the world? (2) Did the Maya really see the end of the thirteenth baktun as the end of the world?

Several famous Mayan experts have challenged the idea that December 21, 2012, corresponds to the end of the world. In their collaborative work *A Forest of Kings*, Mayan scholars Linda Schele and David Freidel insisted that the end of the thirteenth baktun does not signal the end of the world, but indicates a major change in world history, with many events occurring after that date. In this interpretation of the Mayan documents, the 2012 date is seen to be a time of transition into a new, improved age for humanity, not the end of it. Mayan expert Linda Schele has published more than forty books on these subjects. After more than twenty years of careful study of Mayan art, architecture, and writings, Schele concluded: "The Maya . . . did not conceive this to be the end of this creation, as many have suggested." She illustrated her point by citing a Mayan prophecy that predicts events in AD 4772.[18]

Mayan scholar Mark Van Stone pointed out that alternate forms of the Mayan calendar documents do not contain any reference to 2012 as the end of the world. In Van Stone's definitive work on this subject, *It's Not the End of the World: What the Ancient Maya Tell Us About 2012*, he goes to great lengths to show that the Maya did not have a concept of the world ending in 2012. His conclusion: "Life and the calendar will continue without interruption beyond 2012. . . . The short answer from the Maya is, It's *not* the end of the world!"[19] This is especially significant since Van Stone is a colleague and coauthor with Michael D. Coe, who insists that 2012 *is* the end date of the world for the Maya.

Writing for the Foundation for the Advancement of Mesoamerican Studies (FAMSI), however, Van Stone stated categorically:

> There is nothing in the Maya or Aztec or ancient Mesoamerican prophecy to suggest that they prophesied a sudden or major change of any sort in 2012. The notion of a "Great Cycle" coming to an end is completely a modern invention. Mayan inscriptions that predict the future consistently show that they expected life to go on pretty much the same forever. At Palenque, for instance, they predicted that people in the year AD 4772 would be celebrating the anniversary of the coronation of their great king Pakal.[20]

THE DEBATE GOES ON

Despite the impressive studies by Mayan experts like Schele, Freidel, and Van Stone, the controversy goes on between those who say the Maya were making a doomsday prediction for 2012 and those who insist there is no indication the Maya saw that date as being the end of the world. Those of us in the Western world tend to see history as a linear progression. That is, we see events having a beginning, a middle, and an end. Many cultures like the Mayan see history as cyclical. That is, there is a beginning and a middle, but the ending is merely a repetition of the former beginning that is coming around again. As Mayan expert Gerald Benedict expressed it, "For the Maya, the future was believed to be a repetition and variation of what had happened in the past."[21] It is not surprising that many Mayan scholars do not see 2012 as the end of the world, but as a new beginning of human society.

One of the oldest Mayan calendar manuscripts is housed in archives in Dresden, Germany. Professor Nikolai Grube, a Mayan scholar, has been studying the *Dresden Codex* for many years and has concluded that the last chapter of the document does communicate a warning about the end of the world. He noted that it describes black clouds, lightning, torrential rain, and the destruction of the planet.[22]

Former NASA consultant Richard C. Hoagland has done extensive research at Tikal, the capital of the Mayan Empire. He explained that the ending of the Mayan Long Count Calendar on December 21, 2012, does foretell planetwide destruction as the last cycle ends. Hoagland predicted that Earth's rotational axis will be altered, and that the change of Earth's position will result in earthquakes, super-volcanic eruptions, and a colossal wave sweeping around the world, destroying everything in its path.[23]

On the other hand, Mayanist John Major Jenkins, who has done extensive exploration of key Mayan sites and documents, came to the opposite conclusion. Jenkins explained that December 21, 2012, does not signal the end of the world for the Maya, but the beginning of a new cycle in human history. Jenkins insisted that the 2012 date originated in the Mayan city of Izapa, and that it signifies a rebirth of the world at the end of a cycle.[24] He sees it as a time of "transformation and renewal" for the world, not a time of destruction. He stated that he is working hard to combat "the growing wave of fear" being produced by doomsday interpreters.[25]

Dr. Ian O'Neill, a solar physicist, agreed with Jenkins's assessment: "Archaeologists and mythologists on the other hand believe that the Mayans predicted an *age of enlightenment* when 13.0.0.0.0 comes around; there isn't actually much evidence to suggest doomsday will strike. If anything, the Mayans predict a religious miracle, not anything sinister."[26]

The majority of Mayan scholars agree with Jenkins, supporting the interpretation that 2012 was not considered to be the end of the world by the Maya, but a rebirth of the world to a better state of society. The ancient Maya did warn that the transition into that new state may be turbulent, especially if humanity continues to abuse each other and nature.[27]

Modern-day Maya have even been drawn into this controversy. Mayan elder Apolinario Chile Pixtun and Mexican archaeologist Guillermo Bernal have affirmed the "apocalypse" as a Western idea that has very little significance for the Mayan belief system. Bernal asserted that Westerners, who are looking for new myths to explain their world, have forced the 2012 endtime date on the Mayan documents. Contemporary Mayan priest and elder Carlos Barrios complained:

> Anthropologists visit the temple sites and read the steles and inscriptions and make up stories about the Maya, but they do not read the signs correctly. It's just their imagination. . . . Other people write about prophecy in the name of the Maya. They say that the world will end in December 2012. The Maya elders are angry with this. The world will not end. It will be transformed.[28]

Mayan archaeologist José Huchm stated, "If I went to some Mayan-speaking communities and asked people what is going to happen in 2012, they wouldn't have any idea. That the world is going to end? They wouldn't believe you."[29] Many modern-day Maya believe that "2012 is not the destruction of the earth; it's the destruction by fire of old ways that don't work."[30]

Don Alejandro Cirilo Perez Oxlaj, head of the National Mayan Council of Elders of Guatemala, said:

> According to the Maya Long Count Calendar, we are finalizing the 13 Baktun and 13 Ahau, thus approaching

the *year zero*. We are at the doorsteps of the ending of another period of the Sun, a period that lasts 5,200 years and ends with several hours of darkness. After this period of darkness there comes a new period of the Sun. . . . The world is transformed and we enter a period of understanding and harmonious coexistence where there is social justice and equality for all.[31]

Again, a Mayan leader insisted that 2012 does not mean the end of the world, but the end of the present world order and the transition into a new, better one.

CONCLUSION

It does seem that if December 21, 2012, was an earth-shattering prediction for the Maya of the end of the world, it would have been preserved as an important part of the cultural and religious heritage of that civilization, even today. But apparently, such is not the case. Many modern Maya do not affirm that interpretation of their calendar and belief system, but complain that Westerners have forced this interpretation on them from their own perspectives and for their own purposes.

Having said that, even if it could be proven that the Maya predicted the end of the world in 2012, what would qualify them as prophets? Although the Maya were gifted astronomers, that ability does not necessarily mean they were gifted prophets. According to the same logic, do we expect present-day astronomers, who have made incredible discoveries through the use of advanced telescopes and space-traveling satellites, to be qualified to provide us with trustworthy, detailed predictions of the future of our planet? Of course not! The idea that those who make remarkable astronomical observations are therefore qualified to be seers, predictors, and prophets of future events is unfounded.

It may be that the Maya were surprisingly adept and amazingly meticulous in their disciplined studies of astronomy, but that does not guarantee their predictive abilities. Although it seems probable that the Mayan Long Count Calendar does predict a cataclysmic event of some kind in 2012, that possible interpretation does not in any way assure the accuracy of their predictions. They were astronomers, not prophets, and the attempt to use their calendar as "proof" that the end of the world will take place on December 21, 2012, is both illogical and unfounded.

TWO

SOLAR STORMS

Intense solar activity won't begin immediately. Solar cycles usually take a few years to build from solar minimum (where we are now) to Solar Max, expected in 2011 or 2012.

—Dr. David Hathaway of the Marshall Space Flight Center

The young telegrapher sat at the desk for the first time, alone. The seasoned telegrapher, his boss, was taking his lunch break, and had left George in charge. There were no messages coming in and nothing to be sent out, but he felt powerful knowing that he was in control.

Suddenly, huge fireballs from the sky erupted on the far side of town. A multicolored aurora lit up the sky. Fires broke out in the downtown area of the city. The telegraph line went completely dead. George tried to revive it, but nothing worked. George wanted to send a message to other cities to find out if it had happened there as well, but there was no connection with anyone. The whole telegraph system was dead. George could only hold his head and think, *What have I done?* The date: September 1, 1859.

NASA scientists have been studying the huge solar storm that hit the earth on September 1–2, 1859, to predict whether it might happen again. Bruce Tsurutani, a plasma physicist with NASA, called the 1859 event "the perfect space storm."[1] Others have described it as "the most powerful solar storm in recorded history." The 1859 solar storm overwhelmed Earth's magnetic fields and disrupted electrical grids and communications systems. It shorted out telegraph wires, causing widespread fires. Tsurutani revealed, "The question I get asked most often is, 'Could a perfect space storm happen again, and when?' I tell people it could, and could very well be even more intense than what transpired in 1859."[2]

In order to understand the explosive potential of the sun, NASA physicists have explained that the sun is almost a million miles wide. It contains 99.86 percent of the mass contained in the entire solar system. The energy generated by the sun is equal to one hundred billion tons of TNT exploding every second. Given the sun's incredible size, power, volatility, and influence on Earth, NASA officials issued a public warning that a massive solar storm may strike Earth soon. NASA officials called the coming storm a "solar maximum."

Dr. Mausumi Dikpati and her team at the National Center for Atmospheric Research predicted that the next solar maximum would probably occur in 2012. Also, Dr. David Hathaway of the Marshall Space Flight Center stated that the next solar maximum is "expected in 2011 or 2012" (NASA .gov). 2012 enthusiast Lawrence E. Joseph believes studies by solar scientists have shown that "the solar maximum period starting 2011 and peaking in 2012 . . . [may well produce] the catastrophe Mayan astronomers have been warning us about for the past 1,500 years."[3]

CORONAL MASS EJECTIONS

Dr. Tony Phillips of NASA reported that NASA's twin stereo probes orbiting the sun have provided new information about coronal mass ejections (CME). Phillips explained: "Coronal mass ejections are billion-ton clouds of hot magnetized gas that explode away from the sun at speeds topping a million mph."[4] The effect of that much magnetic energy hitting Earth could be the disruption of cell phone communication, electrical power outages, radio blackouts, failure of GPS navigation systems, and computer crashes.

Physicist Dr. Paul LaViolette predicted that coronal mass ejections of sufficient size could move Earth's outer crust and produce powerful earthquakes that would shake the planet, causing incredible destruction.[5] This prediction reminds us of Jesus' prophecy that earthquakes "in various places" will precede the end (Matthew 24:7). We need to keep in mind the destructive power of earthquakes. An earthquake that occurred in Tangshan, China, in 1976, killed more than six hundred thousand people.[6] If immense coronal mass ejections from the sun take place, the resulting earthquakes could kill millions, even billions of people.

SOLAR CYCLE 24 IS COMING

Solar activity occurs in cycles of intensity. The scientists at the National Center for Atmospheric Research (NCAR) have developed a new model for predicting solar cycles, which appear approximately every eleven years. Twenty-three solar cycles have been studied so far. The NCAR team is predicting that cycle 24 "is likely to reach its peak about 2012."[7]

Ken Tegnell of the National Oceanic and Atmospheric Administration's Space Weather Center concurred that we will reach the beginning of a new solar storm cycle in 2012. He predicted that the world's power grids will not be able to withstand the massive solar flares that may be produced, and that such an assault on our electrical system might produce a power outage that could last several years.[8]

CONCLUSION

When all of these facts are put together, it becomes very clear that scientists at NASA, NCAR, and the NOAA are expecting massive solar storms to hit Earth in 2012. Super storms with coronal mass ejections will penetrate Earth's atmosphere, causing electrical system disruptions, computer crashes, and communication interference on a huge scale. Some physicists have warned that coronal mass ejections of sufficient size and strength could heat up the core of the planet and agitate the surface, causing serious earthquakes and destruction. This prediction of a catastrophe in 2012 caused by solar storms seems to have ample scientific confirmation.

THREE

CERN AND THE LARGE
HADRON COLLIDER

*One might be concerned about an "ice-9" type
transition, wherein all surrounding matter could be
converted into strangelets and the world as we know it
would vanish.*

—Dr. Frank Wilczek, Nobel prize–winning physicist

The picketers outside the research facility were becoming louder and louder. Their chant reached inside the office of the European Organization for Nuclear Research (CERN). "Stop the collider! Stop the collider!"

A news reporter asked the head of the demonstration why they were doing this.

"We are afraid," he said. "The experiments they are doing at CERN are extremely dangerous!"

The reporter asked what kind of danger he was talking about.

"Danger of destroying all human life and the planet itself!"

The news reporter asked what kind of experiments could possibly do that.

"They are trying to replicate the Big Bang that created the universe, but they don't know what they're doing. Their collider could produce black holes and unknown particles that would tear through Earth and destroy everything and everyone!"

The reporter approached the car of one of the CERN researchers as he tried to enter the gate, but the scientist said he had no comment.

CERN

CERN is the French acronym for the *European Organization for Nuclear Research*. It was founded in 1954 by eleven countries of Western Europe and now has twenty member nations. The CERN Web site describes itself as "one of the world's largest and most respected centres for scientific research."[1] CERN researchers affirm that their mandate is "finding out what the Universe is made of and how it works."[2] The CERN laboratories are located near Geneva, Switzerland.

THE LARGE HADRON COLLIDER

The Large Hadron Collider, built by CERN scientists, is a particle accelerator and collider that houses two beams of subatomic particles (protons) and causes them to collide at very high energy levels in order to "recreate the conditions just after the Big Bang."[3] The tunnel that holds the operation is seventeen miles long and is buried almost six hundred feet under the surface of Earth's crust. The energy required to produce this collision is immense. Each proton beam has the energy level of seven trillion electron volts, giving a total collision energy of fourteen trillion. The protons travel around the ring of the collider, curved in their trajectory by powerful magnets, until they reach a velocity of 99.99 percent of the speed of light and are forced to crash into each other.

The CERN scientists hope the collisions of protons at that speed and energy level will simulate the Big Bang and produce many never-before-seen particles they can study. They believe the experiment "will revolutionise our understanding, from the miniscule world deep within atoms to the vastness of the Universe."[4] Although they do not know with certainty exactly what will be produced by the collisions, they are confident that the results will change the science of physics. "There are many theories as to what will result from these collisions, but what's for sure is that a brave new world of physics will emerge from the accelerator, as knowledge in particle physics goes on to describe the workings of the Universe."[5]

THE RISKS INVOLVED IN THE COLLIDER EXPERIMENTS

Dr. Walter L. Wagner, a nuclear physicist, formed an organization called Citizens Against the Large Hadron Collider. He filed a lawsuit to seek a temporary restraining order to halt the LHC experiments until serious safety issues could be addressed (March 21, 2008). On his Web site, Wagner stated that the next "accelerator might give us a major step forward in our understanding of the universe, but the risk/reward ratio is absolutely unacceptable if the risk is the termination of Homo sapiens."[6]

Elizabeth Kolbert, a reporter for the *New Yorker*, interviewed Jos Engelen (CERN's chief scientific officer) and other leaders of the CERN project and filed this report:

> Worries about the end of the planet have shadowed nearly every high-energy experiment. Such concerns were given a boost by *Scientific American*—presumably inadvertently, in 1999. That summer, the magazine ran a letter to the editor about Brookhaven's Relativistic Heavy Ion Collider, then nearing completion. The letter suggested that the Brookhaven collider might produce a "mini black hole" that would be drawn toward the center of the earth, thus devouring the entire planet within minutes.[7]

Frank Wilczek, a physicist who later won a Nobel Prize, wrote a response for the magazine. Wilczek dismissed the idea of mini black holes, but raised a new possibility: the collider could produce "strangelets," a form of matter that some think might exist at the center of neutron stars. In that case, he explained, "One might be concerned about an 'ice-9'-type transition, wherein all surrounding matter could be converted into strangelets and the world as we know it would vanish."[8] Strangelets are particles that engulf any matter they touch, making it a part of the strangelet. This danger of the CERN experiments, announced by an eminent physicist who is part of the CERN team, is very disconcerting to many observers.

Even CERN physicist Alvaro de Rújula admitted, "Science is what we do when we don't know what we're doing."[9] Many people have become very upset by the idea that the CERN team does not really know what they may be creating, and that their experiments might release particles that could seriously damage or even destroy Earth.

Some scientists fear that the Large Hadron Collider might produce *black holes* that could destroy matter on Earth. A somewhat dark humor approach to this possibility was voiced in Robert Matthews's *New Scientist* article entitled "A Black Hole Ate My Planet." Referring to the Heavy Ion Collider at the Brookhaven National Laboratory in New Jersey (which is much weaker than the Large Hadron Collider), Matthews wrote, "*Uh-oh*, the mad scientists are at it again. In their determination to extract nature's secrets, physicists in America have built a machine so powerful it has raised fears that it might cause The End of The World As We Know It."[10] Others do not see this possibility as a joking matter at all.

ASSURANCES OF SAFETY BY CERN RESEARCHERS

One of the major causes of these fears is that, although the CERN researchers have assured everyone that they have taken all the necessary safety precautions to avoid an accident, the LHC misfired when it was turned on for the first time. On September 10, 2008, the LHC team attempted to circulate a beam through the machine, but the system broke down when a faulty magnet connection released almost a ton of liquid helium (the project coolant). That kind of system breakdown makes people very uneasy about the CERN team's ability to predict and control the dangerous experiments they are performing.

There are many people who have fears that the collider experiments may well unleash destructive particles that could damage or even destroy Earth. The CERN Research Board has responded to thousands of concerned citizens who e-mailed and phoned them questioning the wisdom of starting up the LHC (and death threats from some even more fanatical opponents). To answer those concerns, the Research Board set up a committee to do a thorough "study of possibly dangerous events during heavy ion collisions at LHC." The committee studied "the possible production of black holes, magnetic monopoles and strangelets." They concluded that the risk of environmental damage by black holes and monopoles was "negligibly small." They also concluded that it would be impossible for the LHC to produce stable strangelets that would be capable of destroying or absorbing matter—"a possibility that has been excluded by the stability studies."[11]

The CERN Web site offers quotes from recognized scientific authorities to bolster their affirmation of total safety and reliability:[12]

- *Vitaly Ginzburg*, Nobel Laureate in physics: "To think that LHC particle collisions at high energies can lead to dangerous black holes is rubbish."
- *Stephen Hawking*, professor of mathematics at the University of Cambridge: "The world will not come to an end when the LHC turns on. The LHC is absolutely safe."
- *Prof. Lord Martin Rees*, astronomer and president of the British Royal Society: "There is no risk."
- *R. Aleskan and the twenty external members of the CERN Scientific Policy Committee*: "There is no basis for any concerns about the consequences of new particles or forms of matter that could possibly be produced at the LHC."

CONCLUSIONS

The evidence regarding the relative safety of the collider experiments is ambiguous at best. The CERN staff and other prominent scientists have assured the public that everything at the LHC is totally under control and that there is no possibility of creating a disaster. Still, their assurances beg the question that if everything is under control, as they say it is, why was there a breakdown of the LHC on September 10, 2008? Further, some of their own scientists have admitted that no one really knows what the LHC will produce when it operates at full power, and a remote possibility does exist of the creation of forms of matter that would be devastating to the planet. On November 23, 2009, the CERN teams turned on the collider and were able to cause two proton beams to collide at the site of the ALICE detector, with no ill effects, although the experiment was not conducted at full power.[13]

Thinking about the inherent risks involved in the CERN experiments, I can't help but be reminded of an episode with a rhinoceros in Kenya that illustrates this point. I traveled to Kenya to visit my sister and brother-in-law, missionaries for more than thirty-five years. They took me on safari in a beautiful game reserve where we saw elephants, lions, cheetahs, and antelopes. But we happened to see a man with a rifle standing near a very large rhinoceros. We approached him.

My sister—the brave one—asked if we could pet the rhino. The man said the rhino was wild, but if we were very careful, we could stroke him while he gave the rhino some food to eat. Before I would get near the animal, I asked the warden what would happen if he shot the rhino with his rifle. His shocking answer: "He would get very irritated."

So, with fear and trepidation I approached the one-ton beast and began to pet him. Unfortunately, I was standing by his head, where I could clearly see his huge three-foot horn just inches from my body. Halfway through the process, I realized that all he had to do was turn his head and I would be impaled on that horn. But I continued petting him, watching for any movement of his head. He never attacked, but he could have done so. That was a great experience, one I will never forget, partly because the risk was so great and there was no guarantee that the worst might not happen. I must hasten to add that if the rhino had turned his head and gored me, I would have a totally different view of that event! Maybe that is a parable for what we face now with the LHC experiments.

In the final analysis, as with every scientific breakthrough that runs risks, we will have to wait and see what happens. The CERN people may make incredible discoveries that will advance physics and our understanding of the universe's origins and mechanisms light-years ahead of where we are today, or they may create substances that will dam-age the planet, and, in the worst-case scenario, destroy it and us along with it. As is often the case, we may just have to put our trust in the scientists running the experiment. They are well-qualified experts in their fields and certainly don't want to risk harming the planet or us. Those nagging questions about safety still remain, however. Unless Dr. Wagner's lawsuit prevails, the LHC will soon be operating at full power and those crucial questions will be answered—one way or another.

FOUR

THE PREDICTIONS
OF NOSTRADAMUS

After a great misery for mankind, an ever greater approaches.
The great cycle of the centuries renewed,
it will rain blood, milk, famine, war, disease.
In the sky will be seen a great fire dragging a trail of sparks.

—Nostradamus, Chapter 2: Quatrain 46 (AD 1555)

I had seen it many times, but this time was different. As his servant, I had often witnessed the ritual he went through every morning. He would pour a basin full of water and sit down in his large chair. He would enter into a trancelike state that blocked out everything around him. I once dropped a goblet not two feet away from him, but he never even winced.

Suddenly, his face would light up as he saw something in the water, something none of the rest of us could see. But he saw it clearly, and he reacted to what he saw by breaking off his gaze into the water and picking up his quill pen and paper. Often he would write feverishly, as if he would lose the revelation if he didn't write it down quickly. But today was different. As he wrote down this morning's revelation, he wiped a tear from his eye.

"Master," I asked, "are you all right?"

He did not answer, but pointed to the paper.

As I read the parchment, I realized that Nostradamus was describing the end of the world, and my body shook with fear.

Michel Nostradamus was a physician, astrologer, prophet, and poet who was born in 1503 and died in 1566. Other authors have referred to him as "the king of secular doomsday seers."[1] He lived during the time of the French Inquisition, when it was dangerous to practice his family's faith — Judaism. His entire family formally converted to Roman Catholic Christianity before he was born,[2] since "conversion in those days was often a matter of necessity."[3] This forced conversion made Nostradamus's Christian faith nominal at best, though he did outwardly practice the Catholic faith with "fasts, prayers, alms and patience; he abhorred vice and chastised it severely."[4] He sought out other expressions of spirituality separate from the Catholic Church, rejecting the emerging Protestant movement as well.[5]

He found his niche in an occult astrology practice based on spiritism and clairvoyance that he believed revealed the future.[6] According to Lloyd Hildebrand, Nostradamus had to be very careful to hide the meaning of many of his prophecies, presenting them as meaningless poetry, because the Catholic Church required "capital punishment for those who engaged in fortune-telling and similar practices."[7]

Nostradamus would enter trances and then look into a bronze bowl of water, where he saw future events unfolding, which he then would write down in four-line stanzas (quatrains). His most famous work, *The Prophecies*, appeared in 1555, and contained the first installment of the total one thousand quatrains published a few years later. *The*

Prophecies were received with mixed reviews. Some thought he was an inspired prophet; others saw him as a demon-possessed heretic. Many Christians in Nostradamus's day (and today) have rejected his work on the basis of a very clear passage in Deuteronomy 18:10–12:

> There shall not be found among you . . . one who uses divination, one who practices witchcraft, or one who interprets omens, or a sorcerer, or one who casts a spell, or a medium, or a spiritist, or one who calls up the dead. For whoever does these things is detestable to the LORD.

Nostradamus would certainly fit within that description.[8] As apocalyptic expert Mark Hitchcock said: "What he engaged in was not a harmless, innocuous, or even entertaining practice — it was divination, which is explicitly condemned in the Bible."[9]

Nostradamus had many admirers during his lifetime, and still does today; but he also has had many detractors, then and now, who have considered his prophecies to be either works of "witchcraft"[10] or to be so vague and confusing that they are useless. An anonymous author published a tract against Nostradamus in 1557, entitled "The First Invective of Lord Hercules the Frenchman Against Monstradamus [*sic*]."[11] He considered Nostradamus to be a monster who had to be stopped.

Michael Rathford, a Nostradamus "believer," admitted

that a criticism of Nostradamus "reiterated through the centuries, is that Nostradamus' 'predictions' are veiled in such obscure symbolism that they could mean anything, and that interpretations are impossible in the absence of precision in language."[12] This observation called into question the authority of Nostradamus's supposed predictions of the end of the world or anything else.

NOSTRADAMUS'S PREDICTIVE POWERS

Many people wonder why Nostradamus has become such an important person for 2012 doomsday enthusiasts today. The main reason is that myriads of people believe his prophecies of things that have already happened proved to be so accurate that they also trust his prophecies about future events. Here are five of his most celebrated prophecies and their possible fulfillment (see Nostradamus101.com).

Nostradamus's Prediction:	Suggested Fulfillment:
1. "The young lion will overcome the older one, On the field of combat in a single battle; he will pierce his eyes through a golden cage, Two wounds made one, then he dies a cruel death." (*The Prophecies* 1:35; published in 1555)	On June 30, 1559, King Henry II of France took part in a jousting tournament with Gabriel Montgomery, captain of the King's Scottish Guard, on the Field of Wars. Montgomery's lance pierced Henry's visor, sending a large splinter into his eye and his brain. He lived for ten days in agony and then died on July 10, 1559.[13]

2. "The blood of the just will be demanded of London, Burnt by the fire in the year 66." (*The Prophecies* 2:51) [Note: other translators insist that the text does not say "66," but "twenty-three the six."][14]	In 1666, a fire began in London that in five days consumed more than thirteen thousand homes, destroying the residences of seventy thousand of the nearly eighty thousand inhabitants of the city.
3. "From the enslaved people, songs, chants and demands, The princes and lords are held captive in prisons: In the future by such headless idiots, These will be taken as divine utterances." (*The Prophecies* 1:14)	Beginning in 1789, peasants revolted against the king and royalty of France. They imprisoned many of the royal families, chopped off their heads, and sang songs of liberty and equality.
4. "From the deepest part of Western Europe, A young child will be born to poor people, Who will by his speech seduce a great multitude, His reputation will increase in the Kingdom of the East." (*The Prophecies* 3:35) *Also*, "The shocking and infamous armed one will fear the great furnace. First the chosen one, the captives not returning, The world's lowest crime, the Angry Female Irale not at ease, Barb, Hister, Malta, and the Empty One does not return." (from Nostradamus's *Almanac*, 1557)	Hitler was born to a poor family. He was a great orator who convinced people to follow him by the power of his speeches. He made an alliance with Japan. Hitler used furnaces to exterminate his Jewish captives (the "chosen ones of God"), committing the worst crime in all of human history, especially against the people of Israel. The words *Hister* and *Irale* in the quatrain are believed by many to be *Hitler* and *Israel*.[15]
5. "The sky will burn at forty-five degrees. Fire approaches the great new city. In an instant a great scattered flame will leap up." (*The Prophecies* 6:97)	New York City is located at 40° north latitude, 73° west longitude. The 9/11 attacks came from jetliners in the sky, causing a huge explosion and terrible fires.[16]

We could go on, but those five should be sufficient to show why so many people trust Nostradamus's predictions. His followers hail him as the greatest seer in human history. Confidence in his prophetic powers has greatly increased in recent years as more and more people study his writings.

PROBLEMS INTERPRETING NOSTRADAMUS'S WRITINGS

It is very difficult to interpret Nostradamus's quatrains accurately, objectively, and authoritatively for three reasons. First, he often used "anagrams" in which letters in a word are mixed up to avoid direct reference to someone important that he might offend. It is, however, difficult to understand why Nostradamus would have to do that to refer to events or people hundreds of years after his death. His most famous alleged anagram is "Napoleon," but Napoleon lived more than three hundred years after Nostradamus.[17] Nevertheless, the anagram supposedly appears in *Prophecies* 8:1, where Nostradamus began the quatrain with the French "Pau, Nay, Loron," which makes absolutely no sense at all unless you unscramble the letters to produce "Napaulon Roy," or in English, "Napoleon the king."[18] One researcher found more than three hundred possible word combinations from the alleged Napoleon anagram.[19] His use of anagrams makes interpretation of his writings very susceptible to multiple understandings and subjective interpretations.

Second, the translations of Nostradamus's quatrains into other languages, and even the compiling of them in French, often evidence "willful manipulations" of the texts to force them to give more specific references to events that have already taken place.[20] Nostradamus's writings suffer the same fate as most vague writings when editors or translators try to make them clearer by changing them slightly. As Nostradamus expert Richard Smoley wrote, "Chavigny [Nostradamus's closest friend and secretary] would edit a collected edition of the *Prophecies* in 1568 (possibly with some alterations to improve their accuracy)."[21] So, it is difficult at times to tell whether Nostradamus actually predicted something in amazing detail or whether those who transmitted his text after the event had already taken place made subtle changes in his writings to make it fit the event more exactly. This process is sometimes called "retrodiction."[22]

Third, as one commentator put it, seeing a Nostradamus quatrain is "like looking at an inkblot."[23] In the famous Rorschach test, people are asked to look at very nebulous inkblots and tell the psychiatrist what they see. Their answer reveals much more about them than it does about the inkblots. In the same way, each person who reads a Nostradamus quatrain can see reflections of moments in history or in the future that he considers significant or personally applicable. Just as there is no right or wrong interpretation of a Rorschach inkblot, the vagueness of Nostradamus's writings make any kind of objective interpretation almost impossible. As Richard Smoley observed, "much of the power of Nostradamus' quatrains comes from this obscurity. It has enabled people to read many meanings into them. . . . Nostradamus was entirely capable of writing clearly when he chose. He very often chose not to."[24]

THE LOST BOOK OF NOSTRADAMUS

The History Channel aired a program on October 28, 2009, entitled *The Lost Book of Nostradamus*, which has caused quite a stir among Nostradamus followers and 2012 dooms-day enthusiasts. The program described the "lost book" as "maybe the most important forgotten work of prophecy in history." The *Prophecies of Nostradamus* is a collection of eighty watercolor images compiled as an illustrated book. Italian journalists Enza Massa and Roberto Pinotti discovered it in 1982 in the Central National Library of Rome.[25]

There is a great deal of controversy over whether or not the watercolors were actually drawn by Nostradamus. His son, Cesar, or someone else could have created them. The content of the watercolors and the interpretations of them promulgated by Nostradamus scholars, however, have added a strong mystical element to the entire debate about the convergence of prophecies of a doomsday event on December 21, 2012.

Nostradamus experts have identified seven key drawings

as significant prophecies of the end times. In the History Channel program, two scholars—Vincent Bridges, author of *A Monument to the End of Time*, and Victor Baines, president of the Nostradamus Society of America—gave their opinions regarding those seven drawings. Here are their interpretations:

Drawing Description:	Interpretation:
1. A burning tower.	1. The 9/11 attack on the World Trade Center.
2. A woman threatened by a blind archer.	2. Impending cosmic doom; annihilation of humanity.
3. A learned man with the book of life and a veil.	3. Our generation: the time of the apocalypse, when all is revealed.
4. A serpent with a crescent moon.	4. The rise of violent Islam.
5. A wild man with a blank book of life, veil dropped.	5. All is revealed and life is over.
6. A tree attacked by a slanted club.	6. The world tilted off its axis.
7. A scorpion with a spiral between its claws.	7. The time of the end of the world will come when the sun aligns itself during the winter solstice with the center of our spiral galaxy: the most exact alignment will be on December 21, 2012.

If you were to put the seven predictions together, they would produce an alarming end-of-the-world scenario:

- The 9/11 attacks on the Twin Towers signal a countdown to the last days.
- The secrets about the end of the world are revealed to humanity.
- Violent Islamic forces wage war against the West.
- The world spins into a period of cosmic upheaval and annihilation.
- Earth is knocked off its axis, resulting in earthquakes, volcanic eruptions, and devastation.
- All life is destroyed.
- The final destruction takes place on December 21, 2012.

If we combine these watercolor drawing interpretations with Nostradamus's written prediction of the end of the world, we would find an interesting, if disturbing picture: "After a great misery for mankind, an ever greater approaches. The great cycle of the centuries renewed, it will rain blood, milk, famine, war, disease. In the sky will be seen a great fire dragging a trail of sparks" (Nostradamus, *The Prophecies*, Century 2: Quatrain 46).

CONCLUSION

It is easy to see why these interpretations of watercolor drawings have been considered by opposing groups to be either the startling revelations of coming cosmic events or else the fanciful creations of imaginative followers of Nostradamus seeking to make his works relevant to our period in history and hoping to ride the wave of 2012 doomsday excitement. Nevertheless, they have added considerable impetus to the 2012 consensus, and are given a place of special honor and authority by many people in the ongoing debate. The dual doubts about whether or not Nostradamus actually painted the watercolors and, if he did, whether or not they mean what some modern experts have interpreted them to mean make this pillar for 2012 less than convincing.

FIVE

THE REVERSAL
OF THE MAGNETIC POLES

Although extremely unlikely, we will admit that it might be possible for a reversal of the Earth's magnetic field to be triggered by a meteorite or cometary impact, or even for it to be caused by something more "gentle," such as the melting of the polar ice caps.

—United States Geological Survey, National Geomagnetism Program

For the navigator aboard the cruise ship *Paradise*, it was a typically beautiful afternoon. The tourists had returned from St. Thomas, and the ship was making preparations to sail north to Tampa, ending the cruise. As John began to set course for the return trip, something unheard-of happened. The ship's compass reversed itself! North was now south, and south was now north. John couldn't believe his eyes. He turned to the captain. "Sir, all of our compasses have just reversed themselves!"

The captain explained to John that he had been warned that the solar flares that had hit a few days earlier might produce that effect. "Earth's magnetic poles have reversed, John. So, plot our course to go south, and we will follow that course to the north."

"Yes, sir," John responded. "Will the flares cause any other problems, Captain?"

Just then, a huge tsunami wave three thousand feet high rushed toward the ship. Before anyone had time to react, the ship had been flipped over and forced underwater. No one survived.

Another of the ten pillars of the 2012 doomsday movement is the prediction that soon there may be a *geomagnetic reversal* in which the north and south magnetic poles (*not* the physical poles) will reverse themselves because of huge solar flares hitting the planet. Jeremy Hsu, staff writer for *Science .com.* wrote an article in August 2008 based partly on the findings of two geophysicists, Mioara Mandea of Germany and Nikls Olsen of Denmark.[1] Hsu explained that something "is changing Earth's protective magnetic field." For years, scientists have observed what they call the "South Atlantic Anomaly." That is, there appears to be a weak spot—located in the southern Atlantic region—in the magnetic field that surrounds Earth. Hsu referred to this as "a dent in the Earth's protective bubble."

How do scientists know that the magnetic field surrounding Earth is becoming weaker? They study pottery! When clay is heated to high temperatures for the making of pottery, "iron particles it contains align with the earth's magnetic field, recording the field's condition at that particular moment."[2] From the paleomagnetists' study of pottery samples taken from various periods of ancient history to the present, it has become apparent that the strength of the magnetic field is definitely weakening.[3] Also, NASA has discovered "cracks in the [magnetic] field . . . [which] can remain open for hours, allowing solar winds to flow into the atmosphere."[4] This is of grave concern to scientists because it is the magnetic field that protects us from the harmful radiation that comes from the sun. Without the magnetic field, we would burn to death.

Lawrence E. Joseph weighed in on the possibility of magnetic pole reversal by explaining: "Earth's magnetic field, or magnetosphere, is generated by the spinning of the planet's core . . . creating a giant electromagnetic field . . . its primary purpose is to prevent potentially lethal incoming solar radiation from reaching the surface of the Earth."[5] He also described current scientific studies about the "South Atlantic Anomaly." It is "a 100,000-mile crack [in the Earth's magnetic field that] . . . opens up over the ocean between Brazil and Africa."[6]

That "dent" has already caused problems with electrical grids in that area of the world, and it continues to grow larger all the time. The break in the magnetosphere means that "more and more cosmic rays are slipping through the Earth's magnetic shield, shredding ozone molecules . . . resulting in greater threats to human and environmental health."[7] Combining the weakening of Earth's protective magnetic field, the possible reversal of the magnetic poles, and the possibility of massive solar flares in 2012 has produced serious concern for many scientists.[8]

According to the *Nature Geoscience* studies, Earth's core acts as a giant electromagnet, producing a magnetic field that extends 36,000 miles into space. That magnetic field has protected Earth from the life-threatening effects of high-energy radiation from the sun. Many geophysicists believe that a similar weakening of the magnetic field produced a reversal of the north and south magnetic poles about 780,000 years ago. Some studies indicate that another geomagnetic reversal may occur soon, but the evidence for that possibility has not been conclusive so far.[9]

Professor Mandea told *SPACE.com*, "If there are magnetic storms and high-energy particles coming from the sun, the satellites could be affected and their connections could be lost."[10] Our communications satellites are especially vulnerable to the destructive effects of the radiation produced by solar storms. Hsu reported that in 2006, a large sunspot produced a large radiation storm that affected satellites observing the sun and caused the astronauts aboard the International Space Station to move to a protected area of the station to "avoid unnecessary radiation exposure (*Science.com*)."[11]

John Rennie, contributing editor for *Scientific American*, described a destructive chain of events that could be created by enormous solar flares, which would change Earth's magnetic field. He stated that if the magnetic field were weakened, Earth's core would begin to move. Huge earthquakes, tsunamis, and volcanic eruptions would occur all over the world. The ground under cities would liquefy and cave in, destroying everything above them.[12]

CONCLUSION

As we have noted, some NASA scientists have predicted that massive solar storms will hit Earth in 2012. Such storms could possibly trigger a magnetic pole shift that would damage the planet and disrupt communications, location devices, and satellites. If Rennie's conclusions are correct, the solar flares could weaken Earth's magnetic fields, reverse the magnetic poles, and agitate the molten core of the planet, causing earthquakes, volcanic eruptions, and tsunami waves. And since NASA is predicting massive solar storms for 2012, this scenario could very possibly come true that year.

SIX

COLLISION WITH PLANET X

This is a dance that will not end until Planet X has passed the Earth, outbound, leaving the Earth twisted and shaken behind it. The Earth cannot escape, and the progress of Planet X will not halt.

—Nancy Lieder, from her Web site ZetaTalk

Nancy was only nine years old when it happened. What looked like a bright light came from the sky and crashed into the field next to her home. Her parents were out shopping, so Nancy was left alone to investigate the strange event. As she crept near the site of the crash, she was terrified to see what appeared to be a space ship hovering above the ground. When a door in the ship opened, Nancy fainted.

When she came to, she was inside the ship, and there were strange beings hovering around her. As she tried to speak, one of the Zetas told her to lie still. A large mechanical arm with a small device at the end of it began to move closer and closer to her head. As the device touched her scalp, she lapsed into unconsciousness again.

When she awoke, she was inside her home. One of the extraterrestrials was placing her gently into her bed. And then he spoke: "Nancy, do not be afraid. You have been chosen from all the people on your planet to be our voice on Earth. We are very concerned about what is happening on your planet. The device we placed in your head will enable us to communicate messages to you for all earthlings. Are you willing to be our link to Earth, Nancy?"

"Yes, I am," she said, with much more calm than she felt inside. As she opened her mouth to ask him many questions about who they were, where they were from, and what they wanted to do on Earth, the strange being vanished. Later, they revealed to her that they were from the Zeta Reticuli star system. The Zetas communicated with Nancy many times, giving her warning messages for the people of Earth, but few people believed her.

Another crucial element of the 2012 doomsday movement is the belief that there will be a collision or near miss between Earth and Planet X in 2012. The origin of this concern is found in the writings of Nancy Lieder. She claims that, as a young girl, aliens called "Zetas" visited her and inserted a communications device in her brain. In 1995, Lieder founded a Web site called ZetaTalk to make her extra-terrestrial messages public. She achieved some fame in 1997 for sharing the Zetas' assurance that the Hale-Bopp comet did not really exist. When the comet appeared and was observed clearly in the sky for eighteen months, Lieder changed those predictions on her Web site.

She still insisted that the Zetas had communicated with her about Planet X, which was four times the size of Earth and would pass very close to Earth on May 27, 2003. The Zetas allegedly told Lieder that a near collision with Planet X would cause Earth to stop rotating for six days, and the physical poles would be moved, producing a change in Earth's magnetic core and a violent movement of Earth's crust.[1] When that event did not happen in 2003, Lieder wrote that the early date was just a "white lie" designed to confuse the establishment and hide the real date from them. She promised that the date would be clarified later. Lieder believes that the establishment is suggesting other causes for the disastrous events of 2012 rather than admit that she is right and that Planet X's collision with Earth will set off the catastrophes:

> The initial approach for discussion of the End Times in the media was to avoid the subject of a passing planet but ascribe a global cataclysm to all other possible causes for worldwide destruction. The first such distraction in early 2007 was the Horizon Project loaded with team members with NASA credentials, who claimed the pending 2012 catastrophes were going to be caused by the Earth aligning with the galactic center. Per the Zetas, the Horizon Project was to point the public anywhere *but* to Planet X, which was very evident for those with eyes to see.[2]

SOME SCIENTISTS CONFIRM LIEDER'S PREDICTION; OTHERS REJECT IT

Other authors have taken Lieder's predictions, changed the name from "Planet X" to "Planet Nibiru," and linked its arrival to the 2012 prophecies.[3] They have based that renaming on the 1976 work of Zecharia Sitchin entitled *The Twelfth Planet*. In that book, based on Sumerian myths, Sitchin discusses a large planet, Niburu, which collides with other planets, creating "all kinds of catastrophic consequences."[4]

Renowned astronomical science writer Govert Schilling wrote a fascinating history of the search for Planet X by highly respected astronomers. He offers insider knowledge about the interaction between scientists as they weigh the evidence and propose working theories about the Planet X phenomenon. In his book, Schilling chronicled the work of astronomer Daniel Whitmire. Measuring the irregularity of the movements of comets, Whitmire proposed that the orbits of the comets were being influenced by the gravitational pull of some large object in space. Schilling asserted that, for Whitmire, "It seemed as though the comets had been forced into their current orbits by the disturbing effect of a massive planet about a thousand times further away from the Sun than Pluto."[5] Schilling also reported that Princeton astronomer Piet Hut agreed "a distant Planet X is also not completely impossible."[6]

Schilling gave a tongue-in-cheek description of the current mania over Planet X and the government's conspiracy to keep knowledge of it hidden:

> Planet X? That was discovered long ago. But NASA is keeping it secret, undoubtedly in close collaboration with observatories throughout the world. The planet goes around the Sun every 3,600 years in an elongated orbit and is currently on a collision course with the Earth. The disastrous portents of that imminent encounter—probably in 2012—are visible everywhere.

Schilling doesn't believe one word of that 2012 doomsday assessment, calling it "nonsense." Rather, he complained:

> Planetary scientists are being driven to distraction by Nibiru. As are archaeologists. And it is not surprising—you devote so much time, energy, and creativity to fascinating scientific research and find yourself on the tracks of the most amazing and interesting things and all the public at large is concerned about is some crackpot theory about clay tablets, god-astronauts and a planet that doesn't exist. And when you try to explain why it is still just a fabrication, you end up on the believers' blacklist as being in the employ of NASA or the CIA.[7]

Many other prominent scientists have spoken out against the Planet X/Nibiru predictions. They insist that there is no such planet and that the claims to the contrary are totally unfounded. David Morrison, senior scientist at NASA's Astrobiology Institute, said he receives twenty or more e-mails a week about the coming near-collision with Nibiru, which he finds ludicrous since it does not exist ("Ask an Astrobiologist," on NASA's Web site). The scientific community seems to be almost unanimously united in their rejection of the Planet X/Nibiru near-collision predictions, but there are still a very small number of astronomers who have championed the possibility of it over the years.

Schilling had one final criticism of Nancy Lieder's claims of extraterrestrial communication. He explained that parallel with those serious discussions among astronomers, Nancy Lieder gave her announcement that "Planet X was on the way. It would pass very close to the Earth and cause a catastrophic pole shift." He reiterated Lieder's story that the Zetas had contacted her in 1997, telling her that the Hale-Bopp comet "did not actually exist." He noted that "after the Hale-Bopp fiasco, around the millennium, Nancy Lieder announced new revelations from the Zetas. Planet X would pass close to the Earth in spring of 2003, causing its axis to tilt by 90 degrees, wiping out 90% of humanity."[8]

Well, 2003 passed and Lieder insisted that the 2003 date was intended to confuse the "establishment." She promised later revelations from the Zetas, and, not surprisingly, received one: Planet X would hit Earth in 2012. This supposed communication from the Zetas to Lieder "immediately attracted the attention of Maya cranks, who have known all along that something special is due to happen on December 21 of that year."[9] Obviously, Schilling has no time for Lieder and her alleged communications from the Zetas.

Others support her revelations, however. Apocalypse enthusiast Lawrence E. Joseph stated boldly that "Planet X, considered by some to be the tenth planet, [was] discovered in 2005 and officially known as 2003UB313."[10] Joseph observed that Planet X is "believed to be about 18 percent larger than Pluto . . . [and] currently lies about three times farther out from the Sun."[11] Joseph believes that Planet X's orbit takes it haphazardly through the solar system and "such an orbit could, theoretically, have unanticipated gravitational and electromagnetic repercussions."[12]

CONCLUSION

Schilling's final comment on the Planet X phenomenon was so compelling that it bears quoting in its entirety:

> So that means there is plenty to do for the debunkers—the archaeologists and astronomers who take a long and skeptical look at the tidal wave of Nibiru nonsense and explain with scientific precision what is wrong with this cosmic fairy-tale. They will have their work cut out in the next few years. And on December 22, 2012 there will be a new pseudo-scientific cock-and-bull story doing the rounds and the whole circus will start all over again.[13]

Nancy Lieder's alleged communications from the Zetas fit squarely into that description.

SEVEN

EARTH'S ALIGNMENT WITH THE GALACTIC PLANE

There is the mysterious center that keeps all the stars in orbit around itself . . . our sun orbits around and moves closer to this solar apex, as it is called. That is, at the end of December each year, the earth is directly behind the sun with respect to this Great Void; our solar system is being drawn ever closer to this colossal Magnet.

— Patrizia Norelli-Bachelet, *The Gnostic Circle,*
   quoted by Willard Van De Bogart in "The Alignment Generation"
   (Earthportals.com)

As a multitude of planets, comets, asteroids, and cloud dust move through space, they form the spiral galaxy known as the Milky Way. In the center of the galaxy lies a massive black hole that has the potential of sucking the entire galaxy into its vortex. The Milky Way galaxy has an equator, just as Earth does, that runs through the middle of its fairly flat collection of heavenly bodies. Astronomers all over the world have used their powerful telescopes and intricate mathematical formulas to predict the movements of those bodies and the relationship between their orbits and that of the solar system. The young man working at his desk is one of those astronomers. As he worked at his computer, he realized that the computer was spitting out a staggering conclusion. In the year 2012, the solar system would align itself with the black hole in the center of the galaxy. He turned to the older man at the next desk. "Could this be correct, or is this computer just acting up again?"

The older astronomer assured him that it was correct. His own computer had produced the same results, but he was not eager to share them unless someone else could verify them independently.

"Should we share this with other astronomers?"

The older man counseled caution. "It is important,"

he said, "that others come up with the same conclusions
we have seen without any influence from us so that we
won't look like maniacs."

The young astronomer agreed, but he couldn't help
wondering what kind of effect the gravitational pull of the
coming alignment might have on Earth, its oceans, and
the magnetic core.

The main proponent of the Galactic Alignment theory as
part of the 2012 movement has been John Major Jenkins.
His most important works on this subject are his *Galactic
Alignment, Maya Cosmogenesis 2012,* and *The 2012 Story.*
Jenkins described the coming alignment of our solar system
with the center of the Milky Way galaxy as "the alignment
of the December solstice sun with the dark rift [or galactic
equator] in the Milky Way."[1] Synthia and Colin Andrews
have described the galactic equator in common terms: "If
you think of the galaxy as a pancake, the plane of the galaxy
is the edge of the pancake and the equator is the line that
runs down the middle of the plane, dividing the pancake
into top and bottom halves."[2]

He insisted that the galactic alignment, when the solar

system aligns itself with the center of the Milky Way and the sun eclipses the center of the galaxy, occurs once every twenty-six thousand years. Jenkins concluded that more than a thousand years ago the Maya predicted the date of that occurrence when they gave the end-date of their Long Count Calendar to be December 21, 2012. Jenkins remarked that it is amazing that the Maya were able to predict such an event without the use of modern tools like the telescope.

Using unassisted observations, the Maya identified the center of the galaxy as "the womb of a huge pregnant being" where stars are born.[3] As the Andrews have summarized it, "December 21, 2012, is the date of an eclipse of the galactic center by the solstice sun. This will interrupt the energy flow from the galactic center to the earth."[4] The Maya were very concerned about the possible effects of that energy blockage.

Maya expert Gerald Benedict described this "galactic synchronization," which the ancient Mayan priest/prophet Chilam Balam of Tizimin predicted: "The Earth and the solar system will be exactly in line with the plane of our galaxy, the Milky Way. The prophecy tells us that this synchronization marks the end of our World age, and the birth of a new one."[5]

The Maya believed that the center of the Milky Way is "the womb of the world, the place where all stars were born."[6] They were convinced that when the solar system aligns itself with that "womb," there would be very serious effects on Earth and its people.

In his book *The 2012 Story*, Jenkins makes a strong case for the spiritual interpretation of the galactic alignment in 2012.[7] Also, in an interview about that book with Mitch Horowitz of *Coast to Coast AM* (September 10, 2009), Jenkins described the Mayan concept of the end of the age as the end of a cycle that leads to "transformation and renewal" as a new cycle begins. He explained that for the Maya, the end of a cycle comes when corruption has become widespread and there is a need to restore things to their original condition. So, although Jenkins is certain about the December 21, 2012, date as the end of a cycle brought on by the galactic alignment, he does not see it as the end of the world.

THE DEBATE CONTINUES: DISASTER, TRANSFORMATION, OR BUSINESS AS USUAL?

It has fallen to scientist and engineer Jiro Olcott to make the connection between the galactic alignment and the end of the world. In his article "2012—Am I Bothered?"[8] Olcott stated: "Our solar system is now on the verge of crossing the Milky Way's plane of the ecliptic [the relatively flat grouping of orbiting bodies at the center of the galaxy]. It will cross in the year 2012. At this point the gravitational influence of the super-massive Black Hole will be at its maximum." He predicted that the results of that alignment, which have already begun, with "hurricanes, storms and earthquakes/tsunamis around the world . . . will reach a crescendo in 2012."[9]

Author Daniel Pinchbeck shares John Major Jenkins's view that the galactic alignment in 2012 will produce a shift in consciousness, not an apocalypse (see Pinchbeck's book, *2012: The Return of Quetzalcoatl*). Other New Age theorists, like José Argüelles, hold the same view of the peaceful and beneficial effects of the galactic alignment in 2012. They see it as a harbinger of a new birth for human civilization, not the end of it.

At the same time, Lawrence E. Joseph and others have proposed a middle-of-the-road view that avoids the idea of a galactic intersection or "crossing," but does insist that Earth is about to pass through a "cosmic cloud" of energy. Joseph described that reality in metaphorical terms: "We are all passengers on a plane, the Solar System, and our ship is moving into some stormy weather—interstellar turbulence to be exact."[10] Basing his conclusions on the work of famous Russian geophysicist Alexey Dmitriev, Joseph concluded that our solar system will soon be inundated by the shock waves produced by a huge "interstellar energy cloud."[11]

Dmitriev described the situation: "Effects here on Earth [from passing into the interstellar energy cloud] are to be found in the acceleration of the magnetic pole shift, in the vertical and horizontal ozone content distribution, and in the increased frequency and magnitude of significant catastrophic climatic events."[12] Dmitriev's theories predict coming catastrophes, but they do not say they will result from alignment with the center of the galaxy or from passing through it. Rather, Dmitriev (and Joseph) are predicting a third option: Earth passing through a huge interstellar energy cloud, with dire consequences following.

Dr. David Morrison, senior scientist at the NASA Astrobiology Institute, has given a decisive answer to the questions raised by galactic alignment theories. He affirmed that there are two issues involved. One issue is "the alignment [not the intersection] of the Earth and Sun with the center of the Milky Way . . . [which occurs] every December, with no bad consequences, and there is no reason to expect 2012 to be different from any other year."[13] ("Ask an Astrobiologist" on NASA.gov). The other issue is whether or not the solar system will pass through the galactic plane intersecting with it in 2012, causing terrible destruction on Earth. Morrison simply answered, "Claims that we are about to cross the galactic plane are untrue . . . the entire 'galactic alignment' scare is pretty crazy" and it is a scare tactic devised by "con-men."[14]

Morrison pointed out that the solar system is orbiting the galactic plane at a distance of twenty to one hundred light-years. He stated:

There is no evidence that we are in the galactic plane or about to cross it. The interval between crossings is about 30 million years. More to the point, there is no physical significance to crossing the galactic plane. The idea that crossing the plane (which might take a million years or so) subjects us to some special forces (or dangers) is just pseudoscience. One lesson I hope everyone will take from the current Internet nonsense about 2012 is that so-called alignments, whether of planets or the Sun or anything else, are no threat and are not actually of any scientific interest. (NASA.gov—"Ask an Astrobiologist")

Galactic alignment of the solar system with the center of the Milky Way Galaxy in December 2012 is a fact (it occurs every December!). Galactic intersection in which the solar system passes through the center of the Milky Way is a myth—it will not take place.

Morrison's pronouncements have effectively squelched any theories about a destructive galactic alignment or intersection in 2012 for most of the people interested in this topic. Morrison's scientific credentials as a NASA astrobiologist are light-years ahead of those possessed by Jiro Olcott, who is basically an engineer spinning out incredible theories about the effectiveness of dowsing for finding underground water supplies and the influence of mystical energies on spiritual leaders such as the druids in certain regions of England.

He believes the druids had special psychic powers because "their body's cells are exposed to a maximum level of energy. The very liquid crystal structure of billions of cells within their bodies resonates with the energy emanating from the fault lines . . . [which] influences their Chakra points."[15]

CONCLUSION

Suffice it to say that Morrison is a member of NASA's Astrobiology Institute, while Olcott is a member of the British Society of Dowsers. The reader is free to choose which authority on this subject is more believable. This author leans most definitively toward Morrison. The alignment of our solar system with the center of the Milky Way Galaxy will occur in December 2012—just as it does every December— with no negative effects.

EIGHT

ERUPTION
OF THE SUPER VOLCANO

The eruption of a super volcano "sooner or later" will chill the planet and threaten human civilization.

—The Geological Society of London, 2005

Peter's briefing at the ranger station in Yellowstone was going great. The senior ranger seemed to have real confidence that Peter could do the job, even though it was his first summer in Yellowstone. He took Peter to each of the main tourist attractions, giving him interesting facts about each one so that Peter could share them with visitors to the park. Finally, they reached the park's most famous attraction—"Old Faithful"—the geyser that spews out hot water like clockwork. The ranger explained that Old Faithful erupts about every 92 minutes, sending up a stream of heated water as high as 180 feet. It puts out as much as 8,400 gallons of superheated water with a temperature that reaches 244 degrees Fahrenheit.[1]

Peter asked, "Ranger, what causes the water to explode like that?"

The ranger's face turned very serious as he quietly said, "Peter, this is something you must never share with our visitors. Only rangers can know it. It would scare the tourists away from the park."

"Okay," Peter replied, "what is it?"

The ranger began, "The thing that makes the geysers go off is a huge volcano that sits under the park. It is the biggest active volcano in the world, and it could erupt at any moment."

Peter asked him, "Is it safe to be here? What should I do if it erupts?"

The old ranger gave a humorless chuckle, "Son, if it erupts, there's not one thing you can do about it. You, along with everything within thirty miles of the park, will be turned to ash. But remember, that's only for you to know. We don't want to frighten the tourists. If they ask about it, just send them to me."

Peter said okay, but in his heart he wondered if he'd ever feel safe in the park again.

The heat source for Yellowstone National Park's thermal springs and geysers is what many have called "the largest, potentially most explosive, most violent, most deadly active volcano on the planet."[2] Some geologists believe that it may erupt soon, devastating the planet. Lawrence E. Joseph described the possible results of a Yellowstone eruption: "The fact is that it could erupt at any time, filling the atmosphere with sulfuric acid and ash and plunging the planet into a nuclear-winter-type catastrophe, savaging economy and agriculture so severely that civilization might never reemerge."[3]

Volcano expert Greg Breining noted that when Yellowstone erupted the first of three times, about two million years ago, it ejected "a block of rock more than eight miles by eight miles at the base, and more than eight miles high—a mountain far more massive than Everest."[4] The destructive potential of the Yellowstone volcano is staggering.

The geologists at the Yellowstone Volcano Observatory recorded nine hundred earthquakes in Yellowstone between the brief period of December 26, 2008, and January 8, 2009. This is referred to as an "earthquake swarm." Volcanic action often produces earthquakes. As the magma empties large underground caverns, the crust above the caverns falls into the cavern, producing an earthquake.[5] The geologists at the Yellowstone Volcano Observatory, however, hastened to add "At this time, there is no reason to believe that magma has risen to a shallow level within the crust or that a volcanic eruption is likely."[6]

Still, super volcanoes pose a real threat to life on Earth. Volcano expert Stephen Self of the Geological Society of London noted that "super-eruptions are up to hundreds of times larger than these [volcanic eruptions like Krakatoa]."[7] The U.S. Geological Survey described the eruption of Mount St. Helens, which killed fifty-seven people and caused three billion dollars in damages, as the "worst volcanic disaster in the recorded history of the United States. The eruption of the Yellowstone volcano would, in fact, be a thousand times more powerful than the Mount St. Helens eruption in 1980."[8]

Self and his colleagues at the Geological Society of London reported to the UK government's Natural Hazard Working Group that "an area the size of North America can be devastated, and pronounced deterioration of global climate could be expected for a few years following the eruption [of a super volcano]. They could result in the devastation of world agriculture, severe disruption of food supplies, and mass starvation." Self concluded his report to the Natural Hazard Working Group by saying, "The eruption of a super volcano 'sooner or later' will chill the planet and threaten human civilization."[9]

Self's colleague, Stephen Sparks of the University of Bristol collaborated on the report, adding, "Although very rare, these events are inevitable, and at some point in the future humans will be faced with dealing with surviving a super eruption." The scientists who did the study for the Natural Hazard Working Group stressed the vulnerability of human beings in the face of a super volcano: "While it may in future be possible to deflect asteroids or somehow avoid their impact, even science fiction cannot produce a credible mechanism for averting a super eruption. No strategies can be envisaged for reducing the power of major volcanic eruptions."[10]

John Rennie of *Scientific American* has explained that

there are also dozens of super volcanoes in the oceans of the world. They have an eruption potential one thousand times greater than the bomb dropped on Hiroshima. He stated that the eruption of those suboceanic volcanoes could produce deadly tsunami waves around the world. Rennie also clarified that if a super eruption takes place in Yellowstone, the superheated gases and ash from that one volcano would choke the air over the United States and bury the entire nation under several feet of molten ash. Further, the cloud of ash and gases would spread all over the world, blocking the sun's rays from reaching the planet.[11] This phenomenon is known as a "global volcanic winter," and it could last for decades after the initial eruption.[12]

The volcanic cauldron at Yellowstone measures fifty miles by thirty miles—"the size of the city of Tokyo."[13] Its surface has started to expand and contract recently "like the chest of a gasping man."[14] The heating up of the volcano under it could be causing this buildup of pressure underneath the cauldron. It is clear that there is "an enormous reservoir of magma beneath Yellowstone" that could erupt at any moment.[15]

Volcano expert Greg Breining asked the sobering question, "As devastating as a Yellowstone super eruption might be, what are the chances it will ever happen?" His answer was: "Very good, actually. Scientists say another eruption is all but inevitable."[16] This is a distinct possibility since the disastrous chain of events precipitated by solar storms in 2012 could actually produce volcanic eruptions because of the heating up of Earth's core.[17]

I was present in Colombia, South America, when the Nevado del Ruiz volcano erupted in 1985. There was no warning. The residents of the town of Armero were awakened in the night to the sound of the lava and mud slide as it raced down the mountain and covered their city more than twenty feet deep. More than twenty-three thousand people died that night as the mud, water, and lava covered their city in minutes. That figure represents three-fourths of the total population of the city. Later, I stood on the site where Armero used to be. I saw a pointed object sticking up out of the mud by my feet. I asked a Colombian friend what that was. He answered, "It is the spire on top of the Catholic church."

If a relatively small volcano like the one that struck Armero can do so much damage and kill so many people, I hate to think of what a super volcano could do. Michael Rampino, New York University associate professor of earth and environmental sciences, said that the death toll from an eruption at Yellowstone could reach one billion people.[18]

THE YELLOWSTONE VOLCANO AND AL-QAEDA

One frightening twist to the super volcano predictions was spelled out in a report on the Madrid bombings of March

11, 2004. According to the Web site ArticlesBase.com and its report "Yellowstone Supervolcano" (January 26, 2008), the Al-Qaeda terrorists who set off the bombs in the trains of Madrid in 2004, left a message threatening to set off a nuclear device in Yellowstone Lake to cause that super volcano to erupt (also confirmed by HomelandSecurityUS.net). That is a sobering thought. The possibility of a spontaneous super eruption at Yellowstone has produced grave concern and dread, but the scenario of a planned eruption brought about by the detonation of a nuclear device in the caldera is even more staggering.

Is the eruption of the super volcano under Yellowstone National Park imminent? No one knows. Reports of increased volcanic activity under the cauldron seem to indicate quite clearly that pressure is building up. But when that eruption might take place is not known. Yellowstone expert Greg Breining commented on that possibility: "What is tantalizing—and a bit alarming—to consider is the timing of Yellowstone's super eruptions: 2.1 million years, 1.3 million, 640,000 years ago. The intervals are 800,000 and 660,000 years. That suggests another explosion is due—and, in geologic time, soon!"[19]

CONCLUSION

Scientists at the Yellowstone Volcano Observatory are keep-
ing a close eye on developments in the park, but by the time
the volcano begins erupting, it will be too late to do anything
about it. As geologist Robert Christiansen of the U.S.
Geological Survey pointed out: "Millions of people come to
Yellowstone every year to see the marvelous scenery and
the wildlife and all, and yet it's clear that very few of them
really understand that they're here on a sleeping giant."[20]
The eruption of the Yellowstone super volcano, and others
like it, is a real possibility in the future, especially if solar
flares in 2012 heat up Earth's core, causing multiple eruptions. This threat is real.

NINE

THE WEB BOT PROJECT

We do a prediction or a forecast of future events based on subtle changes in language as these changes manifest across the internet in usual conversations. As people discuss the rather mundane things of life, they have a tendency to leak out little prescient clues as to what the future will hold for all of us.

— Clif High, founder of the Web Bot Project,
  on *The Veritas Show* with interviewer Mel Fabregas,
  May 5, 2009

Steve turned on the computer to do his daily run of the data collected the night before by the Web Bot Project robot spiders. They had been crawling all over the Internet, collating data on the terms they had been programmed to investigate. But today, there was a new folder in the data. The robot spiders had found more than sixteen thousand entries of the same three terms: "2012 total destruction"! Steve couldn't believe his eyes. Entry after entry recorded the same message: "2012 Total Destruction." He had never before seen a message like that from the Web Bot robot spiders. What could it mean?

He e-mailed his supervisor, "New message in Web Bot folder 60712—'2012 total destruction.' What should I do with it?"

In a few minutes an e-mail reply from his supervisor read: "Run again—that doesn't make any sense."

Steve ran the data retrieval again and then e-mailed his supervisor: "Same three terms appear—'2012 total destruction'; but I widened the parameters and a fourth term surfaced—'doomsday'!"

The supervisor cradled his face in his hands and thought about his three little grandchildren, who might never have a chance to grow up.

2012 doomsday believers have found two allies on the
Internet to bolster their predictions of the end of the world
in 2012. Clif High and his associate, George Ure, have developed a software program that they claim can predict future
events by tracking keywords on the Internet. The software
program uses "web spiders" to search the Internet for about
three hundred thousand key words that have an "emotional
context." It then records the words preceding and following
the targeted words "that reflect people's thought processes."[1]
The use of "bots" (short for robots) makes it possible to do
simple, repetitive tasks many times faster than a human being
can do them. Bots search out what they are programmed
to find and create a folder with the information requested.
Some Web companies have used bots to track the use of pro-
fanity online. Originally designed in 1997 to predict stock
market movements, Clif High's program is now being used
to predict future events in general.

WEB BOT PREDICTIONS

According to High and Ure, the Web Bot program has accurately predicted the following:

- The September 11 attacks (the program predicted
  a world-changing event in the ninety days
  following June 2001)

- The crash of American Airlines flight 587
- The Space Shuttle *Columbia* disaster
- The 2003 blackout in the northeastern U.S.
- The 2004 Indian Ocean earthquake
- Hurricane Katrina
- Dick Cheney's hunting accident

Third parties have not substantiated those predictions as having been specifically announced before the events took place. The Web Bot Project also made several predictions that did not come true. The Web Bot Project predicted that a catastrophic event would devastate the planet in 2012. The project stops short of predicting the end of the world in 2012, but doomsday enthusiasts see its predictions for that year as just another example of the convergence of predictions for the end of 2012.

CRITICS OF THE WEB BOT PROJECT

Critics of the Web Bot Project and the predictions of High and Ure point out that their results are based on self-fulfilling prophecies. For example, when there is so much hype on the Internet about the 2012 doomsday event, there are more hits on the subject by the web spiders that High and Ure use. Far from predicting future events, critics say the Web Bot Project is just reflecting the fears and interests of people who communicate online. They have also claimed that the Web Bot predictions are "so vague as to be meaningless, allowing believers to fit facts to predictions after the event."[2] Here are some typical Web Bot "predictions":

- 2003 — "a major maritime disaster"; an attack on Congress.
- 2004 — an earthquake with rising water;
- 2008 — "the mood of the populace would improve after the presidential election";
- 2009 — a global coastal event; and "government secrets will be revealed."[3]

It seems patently obvious that many of these "predictions" are just like the fortune-teller who looks at a young woman's palm and tells her that she will meet a tall, dark stranger or come into some unexpected money or have a health problem. There is only one appropriate word for that kind of supposed prediction: *Duh!*

Computer engineer Ben Tremblay has summed up what he considers to be the basic problem with the Web Bot Project:

> Being in the computer engineering domain I think I can see where the Web Bots will succeed and where it will fail. . . . Well, essentially, anything "man-made" could be

predicted in some way and anything man has no control over can't be predicted. . . . The more data Web Bots get pointing towards 2012 just means more and more people are publishing stuff about 2012 and the end of the world. Remember, the only thing they can crawl is the internet and what you find on the internet was created by real persons, not God.[4]

CONCLUSION

The Web Bot project can only predict what people are interested in writing about on the Internet. It can't predict future events; it can only register people's interest in future events. Apocalyptic expert Mark Hitchcock humorously remarked: "I would like to see how Web Bot did prior to the stock market free-fall in 2008. If Web Bot predicted that fall, it could have saved us all a lot of money."[5]

As a 2012 predictor, the Web Bot Project is not of much use.

TEN

RELIGIOUS PREDICTIONS OF THE END OF THE WORLD

And the four angels, who had been prepared for the hour and day and month and year were released, so that they would kill a third of mankind . . . by these three plagues, by the fire and the smoke and the brimstone which proceeded out of their mouths.

— John the apostle,
   Revelation 9:15, 18

The Romans had captured the apostle John for preaching the gospel of Jesus. The Romans judged the Christians guilty of high treason because they would not recognize the Roman emperor as Lord. They reserved that title only for Jesus. Many of the disciples had already been killed, but perhaps the Romans took pity on John because he was an old man in his nineties. So, instead of killing him, they exiled him to the small island of Patmos in the Aegean Sea west of Athens. The rough soldiers threw him onto the sandy beach of Patmos and told him to find his own food and lodging on the island as best he could.

"The Lord has sent me here," John assured them, "and He will show me what to do."

Months passed, and John found life on Patmos difficult and boring. One Sunday afternoon, as he sat in the cave he was using for shelter, John was overcome by a visitation of the Holy Spirit and received a revelation from Jesus Christ about the future. As the vision unfolded, John saw Jesus, angels, God's throne, heaven, and the coming destruction of the world. After the visitation was over, John collected what scraps of paper and other materials he could write on and recorded everything he had seen and heard. The pictures his words paint of the end of the world are terrifying.

He saw masses of people in their death throes, great earthquakes, raging fires, darkness from an eclipse of the sun, fearful beasts attacking humanity, plagues, massive peals of lightning hitting Earth, and finally, the triumphant battle of Armageddon, in which Jesus Christ defeats the enemies of God.

After all his writing was done, John thought, *Now I know why God sent me to this place!*

There is a wealth of futuristic prophecies about the end of the planet that come out of the religions of the world. Some are very specific about the doomsday date, but others just give a general description of what will happen when the world ends. Whether general or specific, these end-time prophecies have added fuel to the fire of 2012 doomsday predictions.

2012 PREDICTIONS BASED ON THE CHINESE *I CHING*

Two brothers, Terence and Dennis McKenna, have devised a new mathematical study of the famous five-thousand-year-old divination document *I Ching*, which they believe shows a pattern of highs and lows in world history. Terence McKenna described the *I Ching* as "a mathematical divinatory [future-revealing] tool" and "a centrally important part of humanity's shamanic [mystic medium-produced] heritage."[1] According to Lloyd Hildebrand, the title of the *I Ching* "means book of changes . . . [and its theme is] the dynamic balance of opposites, the evolution of events as a process, and the acceptance of the inevitability of change."[2]

In the McKenna brothers' book *The Invisible Landscape: Mind, Hallucinogens and the I Ching*, they shared their methodology for converting what they saw in the *I Ching* into a mathematical formula that could be used to understand past events and predict future ones. They called the computer program based on that mathematical formula *Timewave Zero*, and claimed that "the software takes these theories and discoveries concerning the *I Ching* and creates time maps based on them."[3] The McKennas identified timewave maps in history showing the novelty of events that caused human understanding to progress markedly, such as the advent of language in hominids, the printing press, the computer age, and the broader use of psychedelic drugs in the past fifty years.

Through the use of this formula, Terence and Dennis managed to find the end date of world history. Terence predicted: "We are soon to be sucked into eternity. My model points to 11:18 am, Greenwich Mean Time, December 21, 2012 AD."[4] Terence insisted that "we arrived at this particular end date without knowledge of the Mayan Calendar."[5] He maintained it was only after his brother and he had discerned the end date from their *I Ching* calculations that they discovered their end date was exactly the same as the end date of the Mayan Long Count Calendar.[6]

The McKennas produced several charts to provide a view of the panorama of *Timewave Zero* calculations from the Big Bang to the end of the world. One of the charts begins time with the Big Bang event and then ends with the final date of December 21, 2012. According to the McKennas' calculations, each point at which the timewave drops down on the novelty scale, something especially significant and radically new takes place in human history. Their belief is that it is possible to identify points of "novelty" (a new paradigm shift of human understanding and consciousness) in past history with the use of their *I Ching* calculations, and it is also possible to predict future periods of novelty that may occur.

THE MCKENNAS' DRUG-INDUCED DISCOVERY OF *TIMEWAVE ZERO*

In 1971, Terence McKenna and his brother, Dennis, traveled to Colombia, South America, in search of the natural psychedelic *oo-koo-hé*. They did not find that drug, but they did find the psychedelic mushrooms known as *Stropharia cubensis*.[7] Under the influence of a psychedelic high, Terence had a vivid experience, which he described: "I had apparently evolved into a sort of mouthpiece for the incarnate Logos."[8] After returning from Colombia, he began speaking in conferences all over the world, promoting the raised consciousness that he believed could come through "the power and promise of psychedelic dimensions."[9]

The content of the revelation Terence McKenna claimed to receive during his drug-induced state centers around three key concepts: the novelty/habit struggle, the coming concrescence, and expanded consciousness through psychedelic drugs. McKenna described all human history as a struggle between novelty and habit. *Habit* is the status quo view of life in which people limit themselves through commitment to rationality and things-as-usual. *Novelty* occurs when people open themselves up to new possibilities, exchanging their normal, rational understanding of reality for an expanded understanding based on hallucination and transcendent spiritual experiences. Like Hindus and Buddhists, for McKenna, true knowledge only comes when a person escapes the bonds of rational thought and experiences the knowledge that comes from ecstatic experiences.

McKenna's concept of "concrescence" is a state of human existence in which:

there will be no boundaries, only eternity as we become all space and time, alive and dead, here and there, before and after. Because this singularity can simultaneously coexist in states that are contradictory, it is something which transcends rational apprehension.[10]

McKenna summed up that ideal state as love: "an unconditional caring, an unconditional affection that goes through all life and all matter and gives it meaning."[11]

McKenna believed that all humanity is being pulled toward that state of being in which true understanding comes through hallucinations and contact with advanced spiritual beings. It is interesting to see how similar McKenna's views are to the classic Buddhist definitions of *Nirvana*, which he had studied. Religious researchers Jim and Barbara Willis affirmed that in Buddhism, "Buddha is now drawing all things into Nirvana, the place with no dimension and no mass, the place beyond all pairs of opposites, the eternal consciousness from which all things come and to which all things return."[12] McKenna's views are a combination of Buddhism, indigenous shamanism, and New Age concepts.

Finally, the place of expanded consciousness through the use of psychedelic drugs is central to his worldview. McKenna wrote, "For thousands of years the visions imparted by hallucinogenic mushrooms have been sought and revered as a true religious mystery. Much of my thought the past twenty or more years has been caught up in describing and contemplating this mystery."[13] McKenna's experiences with various psychedelic drugs convinced him that the only path to full human enlightenment was through their powerful effects.

He described one of his drug-induced experiences, giving his encounter with elflike beings:

> Everybody's chattering, screeching, crawling over each other, clamoring for your attention, and under sufficiently hyped-up conditions, you are able to reply in a kind of spontaneous glossolalia [speaking in tongues]. There's a bit of art in making this peculiar pseudo-linguistic stream of syllables, and when you're stoned, it's an incredibly pleasurable experience.[14]

McKenna thought the use of psychedelic drugs was so crucial for human advancement that he believed they had caused the evolutionary jump from apes to humans: "The critical catalyst that propelled us out of the slowly evolving hominid line . . . was probably the inclusion of psychedelic plants in our diet."[15] At the end of his article "Approaching Timewave Zero," McKenna gave his final appeal:

> You don't have to wait for the end of the world to get this news. You can just short circuit the collective march

toward realization by accelerating your own microcosm of spirituality through the use of hallucinogens. They are the doorways that the Gaian mind has installed in the historical process to let anybody out any time they want out, provided they have the courage to turn the knob and walk through the door.[16]

Terence McKenna died in 2000, but his theories and calculations have lived on through the work of his brother, Dennis. Interest in his hallucinogenic discoveries by 2012 proponents has created renewed attention to his work. Although Terence claimed to have set the end date of December 21, 2012, without any knowledge of the same end date in the Mayan calendar, some of his critics insist that he adopted that exact date only after he had been exposed to the Mayan calendar predictions.[17] Lloyd Hildebrand summed up the McKennas' conclusions in one question: "Will a destructive Apocalypse take place on December 21, 2012, or will we enter an entirely new phase of existence—the union of spirit and matter?"[18]

The McKenna brothers' work has served as one more confirmation for many 2012 enthusiasts that something of epoch proportions will occur on 12.21.12, something never before seen in the world—and perhaps, the end of the world as we know it. Their use of psychedelic drugs as the basis for their theories, however, does not lend credit to their conclusions.

ISLAMIC PROPHECIES OF THE END OF THE WORLD

Although Muhammad never predicted a fixed date for the end of the world, he did offer several prophecies in the Qur'an concerning the signs that would precede the end of the world. He prophesied that the earth and the mountains will be "utterly crushed" (Surah 69:13–15); "the moon will be cleft asunder, lose orbit and be disrupted" (54:1);[19] and "Jesus whose return to the earth shall be the sign of impending Judgement and that the Final Hour is indeed imminent" (43:61). According to Lloyd Hildebrand, Muhammad also repeatedly referred to end-time events such as global burning, severe earthquakes, an eclipse of the sun, falling stars, moving hills, and the sun rising in the west.[20]

Many modern Muslims have accepted the notion that the end of the world is preceded by the annihilation of the Jews: "The 1988 foundation charter of Hamas, article seven, states explicitly that the organization seeks 'to implement Allah's promise' as communicated to Mohammed, that the Day of Judgment will not come until the Muslims have killed all the Jews."[21] Many of the Muslim terrorists firmly believe that by killing Jews and Americans, they are hastening the Day of Judgment when the Muslim Messiah ("the Mahdi") will return with Jesus by his side and establish a worldwide Muslim empire before the end of the world takes place.[22]

Many terrorists even believe that Osama bin Laden is the promised "Mahdi" and they are helping him bring in the Day of Judgment through their violent attacks.[23] According to Hildebrand, one modern Muslim cleric, Safar Ibn Abd Al-Rahman Al-Hawali, used Daniel's prophecy of the end of the world taking place forty-five years after the "abomination of desolation" to pinpoint the date. He insisted that the abomination took place in 1967, and presented this formula: $1967 + 45 = 2012$.[24]

HINDU END-OF-THE-WORLD TEACHINGS

Hindu eschatology teaches that we are living in the final stage of the existence of Earth as it now is — "the Kali Yuga."[25] Hindus see history as a repeating cycle of birth, growth, corruption, death, and rebirth, parallel to that same sequence in the lives of human beings, but on a cosmic level. The Hindu scriptures, especially the *Bhagavad Gita*, describe the final stage of the present age as a time of increasing greed, violence, sexual perversion, chaos, and degradation.[26] According to Hindu tradition, an event will take place called "the Night of Brahman" in which Shiva, the destroyer god, will come to Earth, kill all the demons, and perform a special dance on their corpses that will signal the end of the world. Then Brahman will inhale all physical reality and hold it there for a long period of time. Later, Brahman will exhale the physical world and the process will begin all over again.

So, in Hindu writings, the end of this world is not actually an end, but the precursor to a renewed age to come. The Hindu view of history does not include an actual end time: "Within the framework of philosophical Hinduism, time is circular. It is the ever-spinning wheel of samsara. It has no beginning and no end."[27] The Hindu cyclical view of history is very similar to the views of the Maya, but in Hinduism, the world and everything in it, including every human, "is an expression of Brahman [the creator god]. Such a cosmos can never end."[28]

HOPI RELIGION AND THE END OF THE WORLD

The elders of the Hopi nation have given many prophecies about the end of the world over the years. The theme of the "Great Day of Purification" appears repeatedly in their most ancient writings. That day is described as a "terrible" time "which is just ahead." "Floods, drought, earthquakes and great storms" will precede it.[29] The Hopis see the Day of Purification as the end of this world, but hold out hope that it can be averted if humanity begins to live in peace with each other and with nature. They believe that it will either be a time of "total rebirth or total annihilation," depending on how humanity chooses to live.[30]

Lloyd Hildebrand wrote, "Some prophecies of the Hopis indicate that time will end in 2012, in full agreement with the Mayan calendar's end date."[31] But other prophecies state that there will be a "Golden Age" after 2012 "filled with peace. However, mankind must go through years of great trial, suffering, and persecution before the time of peace and 'one-heartedness' will take place."[32] The Great Day of Purification was prophesied to take place after the passing of the "blue star," which many Hopi elders have identified as the Hale-Bopp comet that appeared from 1995 to 2000. A Hopi spiritual leader predicted that the Great Day of Purification would take place "seven years after the appearance [of the blue star]."[33] That means that the date of the Great Day of Purification would have been 2007.

Many Hopi, however, believe that the "blue star" has not yet appeared. In their view, "according to prophecy, the blue star is due to make its appearance in 2012."[34] The Hopis, who are peace-loving people, see a great holocaust coming in the future, in which Earth will burn and people will suffocate from the heat, and all will be destroyed except the Hopi nation. Lloyd Hildebrand recognized many parallels between the Hopis' vision and Jesus' prophecies of the end. So much so that he asked, "Are Jesus and the Hopis prophesying about the same event—the Day of Purification, the end of all things?"[35] They may well be doing just that.

END-OF-THE-WORLD MESSAGE OF OUR LADY OF EMMITSBURG

On June 1, 2008, Catholic laywoman Gianna Sullivan claimed to have been given a message for the world by the Virgin Mary. In that message, "Our Lady of Emmitsburg" shared several things about the end of the world:

- the appearance of two suns;
- the alignment of the stars;
- a planet coming between Earth and the sun, "leading to tremendous devastation;"
- 60–70 percent of the world's population will die; and
- 60 percent of those who survive the initial destruction "could die of disease and starvation."

The message certainly contains many elements that are similar to other 2012 prophecies, such as the galactic alignment, Planet X predictions, and the death of masses of people. Although the Archdiocese of Baltimore has censured the message communicated by Gianna Sullivan, many

Catholic believers appear to have accepted it as truth. And 2012 proponents have added it to their long list of converging prophecies regarding the end of the world.

END-OF-THE-WORLD PROPHECIES IN HEBREW SCRIPTURES

The Old Testament repeatedly describes the end of the world as "the Day of the Lord." The Hebrew prophets foretold what the Day of Judgment would be like, in very staggering terms, but never say when it will take place.

Isaiah's Prophecies

According to the prophet Isaiah, it will be a day of "destruction" in which "every man's heart will melt" and "they will be terrified [as] pains and anguish . . . take hold of them; they will writhe like a woman in labor . . . they will look at one another in astonishment, their faces aflame" (Isaiah 13:6–8). The prophet quoted the Lord: "I will make mortal man scarcer than pure gold and mankind than the gold of Ophir. Therefore I will make the heavens tremble, and the earth will be shaken from its place" (vv. 12–13).

Isaiah said that on that "day of reckoning" people would enter caves and holes in the ground to try to escape "the terror of the LORD" (2:19). He concluded that "the earth will be completely laid waste and completely despoiled . . . [because of their pollution of the earth], the inhabitants of the earth are burned, and few men are left" (24:3–6).

Zephaniah's Prophecies

The prophet Zephaniah painted a terrifying picture of the Day of the Lord as a day of wrath, trouble, distress, destruction, desolation, darkness, and gloom in which people "will walk like the blind . . . and their blood will be poured out like dust and their flesh like dung" (Zephaniah 1:14–17). He summed up his description of that day by saying that "all the earth will be devoured in the fire of His [God's] jealousy, for He will make a complete end, indeed a terrifying one, of all the inhabitants of the earth" (v. 18).

Joel's Prophecies

The prophet Joel asked, "The day of the LORD is indeed great and very awesome, and who can endure it?" (Joel 2:11). Joel predicted: "The sun will be turned into darkness and the moon into blood before the great and awesome day of the LORD comes" (v. 31).

Nahum's Prophecies

At the end of the world, according to the prophet Nahum, the Lord will dry up the seas and the rivers. The mountains will quake. The hills will dissolve and the earth will be destroyed (Nahum 1:4–5).

Malachi's Prophecies

The prophet Malachi predicted that the day of the Lord "is coming, burning like a furnace." He added that the horrible fate awaiting the wicked is that they "will be chaff; and the day that is coming will set them ablaze" (Malachi 4:1).

END-OF-THE-WORLD PROPHECIES IN THE NEW TESTAMENT

The New Testament describes scenes very similar to those portrayed in the movie *2012* (perhaps not by coincidence) in which fire destroys the earth and the elements melt from the intense heat (2 Peter 3:7–12).

- Lightning strikes the earth, and a great earthquake shakes it (Revelation 6:12; 8:5).
- A burning star falls to earth and sets it ablaze (Revelation 8:10).
- The sun is darkened (Revelation 8:12).
- Famine spreads throughout the earth (Revelation 6:5–6).
- Masses of people are killed by disease and war (Revelation 6:7–8).

- Mountains and islands are moved from their locations (Revelation 6:14).
- People try to hide from the destruction in caves and among the rocks of mountains, but cannot escape it (Revelation 6:15).
- Fiery hailstones and a burning mountain fall to earth and set fires everywhere (Revelation 8:7–8).
- The sun scorches people with fire (Revelation 16:8–9).
- A great earthquake causes the devastation of the cities of the world (Revelation 16:19).

Again, these passages describe the end of the world, but give no exact date when all of this will take place. Jesus told His disciples: "Heaven and earth will pass away. . . . But of that day and hour no one knows, not even the angels of heaven, nor the Son, but the Father alone" (Matthew 24:35–36). That has not prevented some Christian leaders from trying to figure out exactly when the end will come. Recently, evangelical televangelist Jack Van Impe predicted the end of the world on December 21, 2012. Van Impe (who is often called a "walking Bible" because he can recite almost the entire Bible from memory) used the Mayan calendar, the *I Ching*, and Hopi tribal doomsday prophecies to reinforce the end-of-the-world date of December 21, 2012, but also related them to a rapid-fire recital of Bible passages as well. He is convinced that 2012 is either the end of the world or the beginning of the tribulation that leads up to the end of the world.

Many others, like Harold Camping of *Family Radio*, have done extensive, mind-boggling calculations based on biblical prophecies to arrive at the time of the end. Camping, "the building contractor turned radio evangelist," has tried to set the date for the end of the world twice before. Each of the two dates has come and gone with no end in sight.[36] Now Camping has concluded that it will take place on October 21, 2011.[37] Camping said, "We indeed can be certain that the rapture will occur on May 21, 2011, and the final day of the history of the world is October 21, 2011."[38]

Camping and others like him get around Jesus' assertion that no one can know when the end of the world will come by affirming that His statement only applied to those present when He said it. They insist that today, with our greater knowledge of biblical truths, we can do what they could not do. I suppose that explanation covers the fact that those in Jesus' day could not know something we can now decipher, but it does not explain Jesus' statement that even He did not know when it would occur. Pretending to have more knowledge of the future than the incarnate Son of God seems dangerously arrogant.

Christian writer, pastor, and television speaker Dr. David Jeremiah conclusively pointed out:

How could it be, then, that someone will go on record by setting a date for the Lord's return, and then—even though it doesn't happen—people go right on listening to him? People rush out to buy his next book. I can't comprehend it. It is wrong to make such predictions because the Bible says, "No man can know." For that matter, not even the angels know . . . even the incarnate Son of God did not know. . . . To willingly, voluntarily deceive people by doing something God says you cannot and should not do is wrong.[39]

The theme of the Second Coming of Christ, followed by universal judgment and the destruction of the present world to make way for a new heaven and a new Earth, is mentioned many times in the New Testament. It is a constantly repeated theme that runs through almost every book. Dr. Jeremiah wrote:

There are 1,845 references to that event [the Messiah's return to Earth] in the Old Testament; a total of seventeen Old Testament books give it prominence. Of the 216 chapters in the New Testament, there are 318 references to the Second Coming, or one out of every thirty verses. Twenty-three of the twenty-seven New Testament books refer to this great event. . . . For every biblical prophecy on the first coming of Christ, there are *eight* concerning

His second coming. This theme must be of paramount importance for Christian believers to occupy that much attention in the writings of the Old and New Testament authors. Here are some examples of the many references to this cataclysmic event in New Testament writings:

Matthew 24:27 — "For just as the lightning comes from the east and flashes even to the west, so will the coming of the Son of Man be."

Matthew 24:29–31 — "But immediately after the tribulation of those days the sun will be darkened, and the moon will not give its light, and the stars will fall from the sky, and the powers of the heavens will be shaken. And then the sign of the Son of Man will appear in the sky, and then all the tribes of the earth will mourn, and they will see the Son of Man coming on the clouds of the sky with power and great glory. And he will send forth His angels with a great trumpet and they will gather together His elect from the four winds, from one end of the sky to the other."

Matthew 24:42 — "Therefore be on the alert, for you do not know which day your Lord is coming."

1 Corinthians 1:7 — " . . . awaiting eagerly the revelation of our Lord Jesus Christ."

Philippians 3:20—"For our citizenship is in heaven, from which also we eagerly wait for a Savior, the Lord Jesus Christ."

1 Thessalonians 5:2—"For you yourselves know full well that the day of the Lord will come just like a thief in the night."

Hebrews 10:25—" . . . encouraging one another; and all the more as you see the day drawing near."

James 5:8—"You too be patient; strengthen your hearts, for the coming of the Lord is near."

1 Peter 4:7—"The end of all things is near; therefore, be of sound judgment and sober spirit for the purpose of prayer."

2 Peter 3:10—"But the day of the Lord will come like a thief, in which the heavens will pass away with a roar and the elements will be destroyed with intense heat, and the earth and its works will be burned up."

Revelation 16:15—"Behold, I am coming like a thief. Blessed is the one who stays awake . . ."

Revelation 22:20—"He who testifies to these things says, 'Yes, I am coming quickly.' Amen. Come, Lord Jesus."[40]

CONCLUSION

The 2012 proponents have welcomed these religious predictions as further proof that the end of the world is coming soon. Those predictions that pinpoint December 21, 2012, are accepted as another point of prophetic convergence that is coming together to help prepare people for the end of this world. Even those that only describe the end without setting a specific date are highly regarded by the 2012 doomsday proponents because they echo the conditions predicted by other converging nonreligious predictions.

For centuries, many Christians have believed that their generation was the end-time generation, but none have seen such widespread certainty in that belief as we do today. With the regathering of the Jewish people in Israel, the Middle East conflicts with many nations there wanting to destroy the Jews, and the severe weather disasters that have taken place recently, most Bible-believing Christians are sure we are now living in the last days.

ELEVEN

FINAL EVALUATIONS

If these predictions were to come true on December 21, 2012, what would it look like? Here is a brief hypothetical description of the events that would occur on the day the world ends according to this convergence of predictions:

December 21, 2012

As the solar system passes through the black hole center of the Milky Way Galaxy, cosmic powers are unleashed that have devastating effects on Earth. The core heats up, and unbelievably enormous earthquakes and floods sweep over even the largest cities and the tallest mountains, dissolving them into nothing. Planet X passes between Earth and the sun, causing huge solar flares that ignite Earth and reverse its magnetic poles.

That reversal of poles creates havoc by destroying all communications systems. No coordinated efforts to save people can be broadcast, and people wander around in the darkness seeking help, but none is given. The Large Hadron Collider misfires, producing enormous numbers of small black holes that begin to eat up all the matter they touch.

Volcanoes begin to erupt all over the world, including the one at Yellowstone, spewing out hot magma into cities and countrysides, incinerating everything and everyone in their path. The cloud of ash and smoke produced by the volcanoes covers the skies, blocking out the light of the sun.

As Earth begins to disintegrate, huge fiery meteors and giant lightning bolts hit Earth, producing many large-scale fires. Massive conflagrations sparked by solar flares break out everywhere. Most of humanity is burned alive. Almost all of the people who survive the fires are buried alive by avalanches, drowned in floods, or killed by other people trying to reach safety.

There is famine, disease, destruction, and panic everywhere. People try to hide in caves and underground shelters, but they all die there anyway. As the death toll rises, dead bodies litter the streets and protrude out of the rubble of buildings in every city of the world.

Finally, Earth explodes from the expanding pressure in its core, the gases released by black holes, and the gravitational pull of Planet X. Pieces of the shattered Earth leave its original orbit, crashing into other planets and end up as a small ember glowing in the dark of space as a tragic memorial to a once great planet that has died.

Pretty grim, isn't it? Now, the question is, *Do we actually think all of those events will take place?* The following paragraphs offer an evaluation of the likelihood of each 2012 prediction coming true:

THE MAYAN END DATE OF DECEMBER 21, 2012

There is doubt whether this was really an end date or just the beginning of a new cycle for the Maya. Many Mayanists have concluded that it is merely the end of a cycle, not the end of the world. Further, even if it could be proved that the Maya were predicting the end of the world, on what basis can they be recognized as authentic, accurate predictors of the future?

SOLAR STORMS

Reputable scientists are predicting huge solar storms, and some even pinpoint 2012 as the date they may occur. There seems to be almost unanimous agreement among astrophysicists that we can expect extremely violent solar storms in the near future that could become a serious threat to life on Earth.

THE LARGE HADRON COLLIDER MALFUNCTION AND CREATION OF BLACK HOLES AND STRANGELETS

Although no date can be determined for a possible malfunction, the fact that the collider broke down the first time it was turned on does not inspire confidence in the researchers' ability to control it and the black holes and strangelets it may produce. Fear of the unknown can paralyze scientific inquiry, but irresponsible experimentation without necessary safeguards is dangerous, especially given the grim possible outcomes of the collider experiments.

NOSTRADAMUS'S PREDICTIONS IN THE "LOST BOOK"

The whimsical interpretations of the symbols in the water-color drawings of the "Lost Book of Nostradamus" do not give those predictions much weight. Further, Nostradamus may not have even created the drawings. Even if he did, it is difficult to weigh the validity of modern interpreters' explanations of their meaning. The somewhat fanciful interpretations of the symbols in the watercolor drawings do not lend those predictions much credence.

NORTH/SOUTH MAGNETIC POLE REVERSAL

According to many geophysicists, this reversal could some-day occur as the result of strong solar flares, but they are in agreement that even if it were to occur, the consequences for Earth would probably be fairly minimal.

COLLISION WITH PLANET X

According to NASA space scientists, this planet does not exist. If it did exist, astronomers would have observed it long ago. Scientists believe this theory is nothing more than a figment of the imagination of a woman who believes that aliens inserted a communication device in her brain. Although many 2012 proponents have put their faith in Nancy Lieder's theories, the scientific community has little or no respect for them.

INTERSECTION OR ALIGNMENT WITH THE GALACTIC PLANE

Astrobiologists affirm that intersection cannot possibly happen given our solar system's orbit in the galaxy. Earth is not moving closer and closer to the galactic plane; it is maintaining its usual orbit at about twenty to one hundred light-years away from the center of the Milky Way Galaxy. Dr. David Morrison has explained that even if the solar system were to cross the galactic plane, there would be no ill effects from doing so. Further, the alignment of the solar system with the center of the galaxy occurs every December, with no negative results. December 2012 should be no different.

SUPER VOLCANO ERUPTION

This is probable in the future, but no fixed date can be applied to it. The fact that the Yellowstone volcano evidences a buildup of pressure within does give some cause for alarm about this possibly imminent super eruption.

The evidence that terrorists have threatened to detonate a nuclear device at Yellowstone makes this possibility an even greater concern.

THE WEB BOT PROJECT

This software program seems to be registering the instances of people's interest in 2012 and the end of the world, not predicting the future. The use of Web bots to predict the future is unsubstantiated and implausible.

RELIGIOUS PREDICTIONS

Based on the psychedelic, drug-induced altered states of Terence McKenna, his calculations regarding the *I Ching* predictions of "Timewave Zero" ending the world in 2012 have no real value. The other end-of-the-world predictions by Muslims, Hindus, the Hopi, Gianna Sullivan, the Hebrew Scriptures, and the New Testament are very convincing for the adherents of each religious faith, though most of them do not offer a specific date for those events to occur. The end-time prophecies of the Muslim, Jewish, and Christian scriptures seem to share many end-time details in common. The fact that a respected Bible teacher like Jack Van Impe has set the date of December 21, 2012, as the end of the world on the basis of his exhaustive knowledge of the Bible is not conclusive, but it does demand serious attention. In light of Jesus' teaching that no one knows when the end of the world will take place (Matthew 24), it is surprising that Van Impe and others would make such a claim.

WILL THE WORLD END IN 2012?

In conclusion, the most probable end-time events are massive solar storms, the malfunction of the Large Hadron Collider, the reversal of Earth's magnetic poles, the eruption of super volcanoes, and those events prophesied in the various religious groups' scriptures. Except for the solar storms, none of these predictions carry the exact date of 2012, but they are nevertheless very possible, and in some cases, even probable. Their fulfillment would bring dire consequences to the planet and to all human life. The possible scenario of fires from solar storms and volcanic eruptions, the production of black holes and strangelets sucking up any matter they touch, and the religious prophecies concerning the destruction of Earth and the annihilation of all humanity are certainly frightening to contemplate.

So the answer to the question in the title of this book, *Will the World End in 2012?*, is: it could, but it might not. The world will not end in 2012 *because of*

- that date on *the Mayan calendar*. It is not a date for the end of the world, but the date of transition to a new age.

- the predictions of *Nostradamus*. His predictions are vague at best.
- a *collision with Planet* X. Planet X doesn't exist.
- the *galactic alignment*. It is harmless.
- the *Web Bot Project* predictions. The project only records interest in certain topics by Internet users. It cannot predict the future.

But the world *could* end in 2012 *if*

- massive solar flares and coronal mass ejections hit Earth in 2012, breaking through a weakened magnetic field and heating up the crust and the core of the planet. They could trigger gigantic earthquakes, fissures, and tsunami waves that could sweep across the globe, destroying everything in their path.
- a major malfunction of the Large Hadron Collider produces black holes and strangelets that bore through Earth, destroying all matter as they go.
- the Yellowstone super volcano and dozens of other super volcanoes erupt because of the overheating of Earth's core by solar radiation.
- Jesus Christ returns to Earth, judges the wicked,

and destroys the planet to create a new heaven
and a new earth.

Is there any hope for us if any of those things take place?
What can we do?
How can we be ready for it?

TWELVE

PREPARATION FOR THE END OF THE WORLD

But look at it this way: nothing less than an omnipotent deity could help us out of the predicament that the 2012 prophets say we're in, so what other choice is there for us than to drop to our knees?

—Lawrence E. Joseph, *Apocalypse 2012*, 224

WHAT CAN WE DO ABOUT THE END OF THE WORLD?

Is there some way we can survive it?

Are there precautions we can take to save our lives?

In many parts of the world, 2012 doomsday believers have set about preparing for the end of the world. Bunkers have been built. Abandoned missile silos are being purchased and renovated. Underground shelters of all kinds have been constructed by those convinced that the world will end in 2012. Provisions have been stockpiled, and elaborate plans have been made for sealing up entrances to keep others out. A select group of people have made extensive preparations so they will be able to emerge years after the doomsday event, repopulate Earth, and begin a new civilization.[1] But will they really be safe? Probably not.

Massive concrete bunkers and thick metal walls would not stop the effect of the predicted catastrophes. Whether we consider the effects of black holes from the CERN collider, or solar storms from the sun, or gigantic super volcanic eruptions, or violent massive earthquakes, no bunker would be able to withstand that kind of devastation. So, what are we to do? Maybe our preparation for the end of the world needs to take a totally different path.

Millions of people have already had to face a virtual end-of-the-world experience when they confronted their own deaths.

For them, the end of the world had come as an end to *their* world. How have people managed to cope with the frightening encounter with death? Is there a way to prepare for it?

Your own personal "end of the world" may come in 2012 or 2032 or tomorrow. As we survey the annals of history, we find a group of countless people who have been able to face death with confidence, dignity, and hope. Many of them were imprisoned, tortured, and killed in gruesome ways, while others died of natural causes, but they dealt with death with the courage, the hope, and the confidence that they were stepping into a far better world than this one. The founder of this group even prayed for those who were killing Him: "Father, forgive them." And, as He breathed His last breath, He said: "Father, into Your hands I commit My spirit" (Luke 23:34, 46). How could he have done that? How could a person ask God to forgive those who were torturing and killing Him and in the moment of His death, confidently place His spirit in the hands of God? What an incredible person He must have been! Of course, that person was Jesus Christ!

Not only Jesus, but also one of His earliest followers, Stephen, faced death with a supernatural confidence that must have shaken those who stoned him. He prayed for them as they threw the stones: "Lord, do not hold this sin against them!" Stephen looked up into the sky and "saw the glory of God, and Jesus standing at the right hand of God." He died saying, "Lord Jesus, receive my spirit" (Acts 7:55, 59, and 60).

Millions of Christians throughout the ages have shared Stephen's death experience. They have faced death with an irrepressible confidence and an otherworldly joy that has confused and bewildered their executioners. Even those who have died of natural causes have left a legacy of faith and joy at their moment of passing. Many of them have surprised loved ones by exclaiming that they see Jesus coming for them, and have died with His praise on their lips.

It *is* possible to face your own personal "end of the world" with hope and faith and even joy. The testimony of millions of Christians throughout the past twenty centuries has proven the genuineness of their hope and the depth of their faith in Jesus Christ. You can have that hope and that confidence, too, whether the world ends for you in 2012 or tomorrow. You *can* face the end with courage and hope and even joy if Jesus Christ is your personal Lord and Savior and heaven is your ultimate destination. The best antidote for the fear and dread that the 2012 predictions can cause is to begin a personal, intimate relationship with Jesus Christ, the Lord of time and the Victor over death itself.

THREE SIMPLE STEPS

Beginning a personal relationship with Jesus Christ is not hard to do. Three simple steps will bring you into a life of joy and hope that nothing, not even death, can take away. The three steps are: believe, admit, and ask.

Step 1: BELIEVE

To begin a personal relationship with Jesus Christ, you must believe certain facts. You must be convinced that the Christian faith is true and that the Bible is the Word of God. Otherwise, it will be impossible to reach out to Jesus in faith and assurance that He will answer you.

The Christian faith is true, not because Christians say it is, but because of ample proofs that it is from God and works the way Jesus said it would. The authors of the New Testament were either eyewitnesses of the events they recorded or they had verified the events with eyewitnesses. Eyewitness testimony is a powerful basis for belief that something took place. The consistent testimony of many eyewitnesses is even stronger. But the eyewitness testimony of people who are willing to give their lives for what they have written when they are offered life if they will recant, is the most powerful testimony of all. The Christian faith is true, and its truth rests on reliable eyewitness testimony by those who gave their lives for their faith. As you begin to live in agreement with the principles of the Christian faith and see God work in your life, you will have no doubts about its power and its integrity.

Is the Bible really the Word of God? There are many evidences that the Bible is God's revealed Word. Here are just a few:

- The consistency of its message, written by forty different authors over a period of more than fifteen hundred years
- The amazing number of fulfilled prophecies it contains
- The archaeological confirmation of the Bible's historical descriptions
- The power of eyewitness testimony

Once you have settled in your mind and heart that the Christian faith is true and that the Bible is the Word of God, you are ready to go on to establish your beliefs about who Jesus is:

- Jesus is the Son of God—God coming to Earth to live with us.
- Jesus existed in equality with God before He created Earth.
- Jesus lived a perfect human life and performed wonderful miracles out of love for people who were suffering.

- Jesus took your sins upon Himself when He was crucified on the cross and made them His own so that He could pay the penalty for them by dying in place of you.
- Jesus wants to have a personal relationship with you that will give you love, joy, and peace.
- Jesus rose again from the dead so that He could live in you forever.

If you find it difficult to accept these truths about Jesus, read the New Testament and talk to a Bible-believing pastor about any doubts you may have. If you are to come to Jesus, you must see Him for who He really is and trust Him with your life.

Step 2: ADMIT

Have you ever done anything wrong? Of course you have. We all have. Every single one of us has known that certain things were not right, but we have done them anyway. We have all violated our consciences and decided to do things we knew were wrong. The Bible calls that *sin*, and our sins separate us from God. God's Word says, "If we confess [admit] our sins, He [God] is faithful and righteous to forgive us our sins" (1 John 1:9). Are you ready to take the second step toward a personal relationship with Jesus Christ? Right now, tell God you agree with Him that you have sinned.

Step 3: **ASK**

The final step in beginning a personal relationship with Jesus is just to ask Him for it.

- Ask Jesus to forgive your sins, come into your life, and live in you forever.
- Ask Him to be your Lord and Savior.
- Ask Jesus to begin to change you into the person He wants you to be and use your life to serve Him.

And thank Him for His great love for you that caused Him to give His life for you.

It may help to meet with someone who already knows Jesus personally who can pray with you as you invite Jesus into your life. I shared these steps with a university student, who asked me what he should do about it. I suggested he leave the room, find a quiet place, and speak to Jesus out loud, asking Him to come into his life, forgive his sins, and make him a new person. He left, and about ten minutes later, he came back with tears streaming down his cheeks and a smile lighting up his face. "He did it!" he said. "Jesus came into my life, and I have never felt so clean inside before!" He can do that for you, too, if you'll just ask Him.

After you start your life with Jesus, find a church that faithfully preaches and teaches the Bible and believes in a personal relationship with Jesus. They will help you build a great relationship with Him—one that will guarantee you will never fear the future again, no matter what happens!

So, is the world really going to end in 2012? Jesus said that no one knows when that will happen (Matthew 24:36). But whenever it does happen, you can be ready for it if you belong to Jesus Christ and He lives in you! You can face the future—and whatever it may hold—with unshakable joy and confidence and hope if Jesus is your Lord and heaven is your eternal home. Before His death and resurrection, Jesus turned to His disciples and said:

> Do not let your heart be *troubled*; believe in God, believe also in Me. In My Father's house are many dwelling places; if it were not so, I would have told you; for I go to prepare a place for you. If I go and prepare a place for you, I will come again and receive you to Myself, that where I am, there you may be also. . . . *Peace* I leave with you; *My peace* I give to you; not as the world gives do I give to you. Do not let your heart be *troubled*, nor let it be *fearful*. (John 14:1–3, 27, emphasis added)

If you have invited Jesus to be your Lord and Savior, those promises are for *you*! You never need to be troubled or fearful again about *anything*. Those are great promises whether you are facing the end of the world or the end of *your* world in death. Jesus is waiting to take you to His home in heaven, and no one can take that away from you! Please use these 2012 doomsday predictions as an opportunity to settle the question of your future once and for all. We may not know what the future holds, but we know who holds the future — Jesus Christ! As Corrie ten Boom, a Christian who survived the Nazi death camps and forgave her torturers, said: "Never be afraid to trust an unknown future to a known God."[2]

God bless you as you begin your life with Jesus Christ and enjoy the fellowship, encouragement, and joy of being part of the family of God, worshipping Him, walking with Him, and winning others to Him!

EPILOGUE FOR CHRISTIANS

I WOULD LIKE TO SHARE ONE PARTING WORD WITH THE readers of this book who are already Christians. In his second epistle, Peter wrote:

> But the day of the Lord will come like a thief, in which the heavens will pass away with a roar and the elements will be destroyed with intense heat, and the earth and its works will be burned up. Since all these things are to be destroyed in this way, what sort of people ought you to be in holy conduct and godliness, looking for and hastening the coming of the day of God, because of which the heavens will be destroyed by burning, and the elements will melt with intense heat! (2 Peter 3:10–12)

In other words, Peter was saying that the *best preparation for holocaust is holiness.*

As the end of the world approaches, either in 2012, 2032, or tomorrow, Christians are called by God to be ready for it at all times by living a holy, godly life. We need to be constantly asking ourselves, *Would I want Jesus to return and find me in this place, doing these things, thinking these thoughts, or speaking these words?* Jesus can change us by His power and His grace. If we allow the Holy Spirit to work in our lives, He can transform us into the people God wants us to be.

One day He will come, as the Scriptures say, and "for this reason, you also must *be ready*; for the Son of Man is coming at an hour when you do not think He will" (Matthew 24:44, emphasis added). The best way to be ready to greet the Lord with open arms is to live the way He has commanded us to live and avoid those things that displease Him. We are His bride, the Church, and some day He will come for us. Will we be ready? John wrote, "Let us rejoice and be glad and give the glory to Him [God], for the marriage of the Lamb has come and His bride *has made herself ready*" (Revelation 19:7, emphasis added).

Dr. David Jeremiah wrote, "Because we know the Lord could come today or tomorrow, we pack everything we can into the day God has given us. . . . When you know that just around the corner everything will be resolved, you can live your life wide open for the Lord, always anticipating, always looking for His momentary return."[1] We can face tomorrow with faith and trust and obedience from the heart when we believe firmly that Jesus could come at any moment and take us to be with Him.

I truly believe that this 2012 phenomenon is a wake-up call, not just for the unconverted, but for believers as well. We need to take these sobering predictions about the possible end of the world as an opportunity to examine our lives and make sure we are really walking "in holy conduct and godliness." He could come in 2012 or He could come tomorrow, but the question is, are you ready to receive Him and be received by Him?

- What would happen if all of the Christians in the world acted as if the world were going to end in 2012?
- How would we live out our faith?
- What would be our priorities?
- How would we witness to our lost friends, family members, and acquaintances?
- What would we do with our time and our resources?
- What would change in our lives to bring us to that "holy conduct and godliness" that Peter said is the best preparation for the end of the world?

- What things that now seem so important would become trivial in the light of that date?
- And what things that we now consider to be secondary would become primary in our lives?

Perhaps that challenge will turn out to be the greatest blessing the 2012 movement offers to us as Christians! Of course, the other blessing of the 2012 movement is the great opportunity it offers us to speak to our neighbors, friends, and relatives with love and concern about how to escape the fear and dread of the end of the world by putting their faith in Christ to save them and take them to heaven when they die.

Also, we need to ask ourselves how we are preparing for the end of *our* world, that is, our death. Do we face the inevitability of death with confidence, peace, and even joy — or with fear and dread? Remember Jesus' great words of promise and hope found in John 14:1–3:

Do not let your heart be *troubled*; believe in God, believe also in Me. In My Father's house are many dwelling places; if it were not so, I would have told you; for I go *to prepare a place for you*. If I go and prepare a place for you, I will come again and receive you to Myself, *that where I am, there you may be also.* (emphasis added)

What greater hope could we ever hear than that?

For many of us, the clearest testimony of our faith in Jesus Christ that we will ever give will take place in the last moments of our lives. That was true for my mother. To my knowledge, she never led anyone into a personal relationship with Christ during her life. She invited people to church, sang in the choir, and taught children's Sunday school, but she never prayed with someone to receive Christ. She became very ill, and the doctor told us it was inoperable cancer. As my family and I visited her in the hospital during her last days, we joked with her and she joked right back. Our laughter and joy could be heard all over that floor of the hospital.

One day, the nurse who was caring for my mother took me aside and asked, "Do you people know how serious your mother's condition is?"

"Yes," I said, "we know that if the Lord doesn't intervene, she will die soon."

With a fiery look in her eyes, the nurse asked, "Then, tell me, why are you all so happy?"

I tried to explain to her that we would miss my mom if she died, but we were absolutely sure that we would see her again in heaven. I even told her to look for the mansion in heaven full of laughter—that would be ours! She just shook her head and left the room.

My mother did die, and as I entered the pulpit to preach her funeral sermon, I noticed her oncologist and the nurse I had talked with sitting together on the front row. After the service, I told them how pleased I was to see them at my mom's funeral and how much I appreciated their coming when they must deal with the death of so many cancer patients. The doctor, who was a Christian, said he often attends his patients' funeral services as kind of a last good-bye to them. But the nurse looked at me with tears in her eyes and said, "Many people have talked to me about giving my life to Christ, but I resisted all of them. But when I saw your mother going through such terrible pain with joy and hope and confidence of her home in heaven, I couldn't resist anymore. I gave my life to Christ!"

That is the way a Christian is supposed to face death, and God can use that kind of faith, hope, and joy to bring many people to a saving relationship with Christ. Jesus can prepare us to trust Him in that moment and give up our lives with the bedrock hope of eternal life with Him in heaven. Just ask Him to give you that assurance, trust, and hope, and He will!

He is coming! And we want to be found doing His will so that with joy and confidence and complete assurance of hope we can echo the words of the great apostle John: "Amen. Come, Lord Jesus" (Revelation 22:20).

Lord, help us to be found doing Your will when You come, in every single area of our lives, and give us Your power and Your grace to meet death with praise on our lips, joy on our faces, and victory in our hearts.

In Jesus' precious name. Amen.

NOTES

Introduction

1. See Web site: Breaking Through to God: "Prediction Addiction."
2. See the *Boston Globe* article at http://www.boston.com/bostonglobe/editorial_opinion/oped/articles/2009/07/20/the_end_is_near/.
3. J. Barton Payne, *Encyclopedia of Biblical Prophecy* (New York: Harper, 1973), v.
4. John L. Petersen, *A Vision for 2012: Planning for Extraordinary Change* (Golden, CO: Fulcrum, 2008), 15–28.
5. Lawrence E. Joseph, *Apocalypse 2012: A Scientific Investigation into Civilization's End* (New York: Broadway, 2008), 176.
6. Michael Drosnin, *The Bible Code* (New York: Touchstone, 1997), 1.
7. Jim Willis and Barbara Willis, *Armageddon Now: The End of the World from A to Z* (Canton, MI: Visible Ink Press, 2006), 64.
8. Ibid., 67 (See also Drosnin's second book, *Bible Code II*).
9. Drosnin, *The Bible Code*, 230.
10. Mark Hitchcock, *2012, the Bible, and the End of the World* (Eugene, OR: Harvest House, 2009), 85; and Synthia Andrews and Colin Andrews, *The Complete Idiot's Guide to 2012* (New York: Alpha, 2008), 172.
11. Hitchcock, *2012*, 88.

12. For a full explanation of Argüelles's Harmonic Convergence theory, see http://www.earthportals.com/Portal_Messenger/9hcproc.html.
13. Hitchcock, *2012*, 17; and Andrews and Andrews, *The Complete Idiot's Guide to 2012*, 153.
14. Hitchcock, *2012*, 24.
15. "Thousands Expect Apocalypse in 2012," http://news.aol.com/story/_a/thousands-expect-apocalypse-in-2012/20080706152409990.
16. Joseph, *Apocalypse 2012*, 208.
17. See the entire text at http://www.abovetopsecret.com/forum/thread427727/pg1.
18. For further information, visit their Web site at *www.instituteforhumancontinuity.org*.
19. Hitchcock, *2012*, 59.
20. See http://www.delusionresistance.org/christian/larry/larry09.html for the entire song.
21. Lloyd Hildebrand, *2012: Is This the End?*(Alachua, FL: Bridge-Logos, 2009), xi.

Chapter One: The Mayan Factor

1. Michael D. Coe, *The Maya: Ancient Peoples and Places*, 7th edition. (London: Thames & Hudson, 2005), 46.
2. Andrews and Andrews, *The Complete Idiot's Guide to 2012*, 10.
3. Benedict, *The Mayan Prophecies for 2012*, (n.p.: Watkins, 2008), 12.
4. Ibid., 11.
5. Ibid., 96.
6. *Popul Vuh: Literal Translation*, by Allen J. Christenson, lines 2442–503.
7. Hitchcock, *2012*, 32.
8. Ibid., 31.
9. Ibid.
10. Linda Schele and David Freidel, *A Forest of Kings: The Untold Story of the Ancient Maya* (New York: William Morrow & Co., 1990), 79–82.
11. Hitchcock, *2012*, 29.
12. See his classic work *The Maya: Ancient Peoples and Places*.
13. Andrews and Andrews, *The Complete Idiot's Guide to 2012*, 43–44.

14. John Major Jenkins, *Maya Cosmogenesis 2012* (Rochester, VT: Bear & Company, 1998), 317.
15. Hitchcock, *2012*, 41.
16. Stephanie South, *2012: Biography of a Time Traveler* (Franklin Lakes, NJ: New Page, 2009).
17. Found in the article "Messenger of the Law of Time" at http://www.13moon.com/Votan-bio.htm, and substantiated in Andrews and Andrews, *The Complete Idiot's Guide to 2012*, 167.
18. Schele and Freidel, *A Forest of Kings*, 82
19. Mark Van Stone, on the Web site of the Foundation for the Advancement of Mesoamerican Studies, "It's Not the End of the World." (http://www.famsi.org/research/vanstone/2012/faq.html#13).
20. See Mark Van Stone's illuminating article on the the Mayans on the FAMSI Web site, under the title, "2012 FAQ."
21. Benedict, *The Mayan Prophecies*, 22.
22. Grube stated this on the National Geographic Channel documentary "2012: Countdown to Armageddon."
23. Hoagland made these predictions on the SyFy Channel's documentary "2012: Startling New Secrets."
24. Jenkins, *Maya Cosmogenesis 2012*, 315.
25. SyFy Channel's "2012: Startling New Secrets."
26. For O'Neill's full text, go to *www.universetoday.com/2008/05/19/no-doomsday-in-2012/*.
27. John Major Jenkins, *The 2012 Story: The Myths, Fallacies, and Truth Behind the Most Intriguing Date in History* (New York: Tarcher, 2009), 369–70.
28. Benedict, *The Mayan Prophecies*, 135.
29. Stated by Huchm on the National Geographic Channel documentary "Countdown to Armageddon."
30. Andrews and Andrews, *The Complete Idiot's Guide to 2012*, 35.
31. Jenkins, *The 2012 Story*, 369.

Chapter Two: Solar Storms

1. NASA's Jet Propulsion Laboratory, "NASA Scientist Dives into Perfect Space Storm," NASA, October 24, 2003, http://www.nasa.gov/vision/universe/solarsystem/perfect_space_storm.html.

2. Ibid.

3. Joseph, *Apocalypse 2012*, 101.

4. Tony Phillips, "The Surprising Shape of Solar Storms," NASA, April 14, 2009. http://science.nasa.gov/headlines/y2009/14apr_3dcme.htm.

5. Paul A. LaViolette, *Earth Under Fire* (Rochester, VT: Bear & Company, 2005), 384.

6. Amos Nur, *Apocalypse: Earthquakes, Archaeology, and the Wrath of God* (Princeton: Princeton University Press, 2008), 142.

7. "Scientists Issue Unprecedented Forecast of Next Sunspot Cycle" UCAR, March 6, 2006, http://www.ucar.edu/news/releases/2006/sunspot.shtml.

8. Stated on the SyFy Channel's documentary (Princeton: Princeton University Press, 2008), "2012: Startling New Secrets."

Chapter Three: CERN and the Large Hadron Collider

1. "CERN in a nutshell," http://public.web.cern.ch/Public/en/About/About-en.html

2. Ibid.

3. "LHC milestone triple jump," CERN, http://public.web.cern.ch/public/en/Spotlight/Spotlight3Jump-en.html.

4. "Brussels Train Passes Through CERN," CERN, page no longer available.

5. "The Large Hadron Collider," http://public.web.cern.ch/public/en/LHC/LHC-en.html.

6. Quote taken from Wagner's Web site: http://www.lhcdefense.org/lhc_experts4.php.

7. Elizabeth Kolbert, "Crash Course," *New Yorker*, May 14, 2007, http://www.newyorker.com/reporting/2007/05/14/070514fa_fact_kolbert?currentPage=all.

8. Ibid.

9. BBC, "The Six Billion Dollar Experiment" (LHC documentary).

10. Robert Matthews, "A black hole ate my planet," *New Scientist*, August 28, 1999, http://www.newscientist.com/article/mg16322014.700-a-black-hole-ate-my-planet.html?full=true.

11. Official Minutes of the CERN Research Board, February 6, 2003.

12. http://public.web.cern.ch/public/en/LHC/Safety-en.html.

13. "Two circulating beams bring first collisions in the LHC," November 23, 2009, CERN, http://press.web.cern.ch/press/PressReleases/Releases2009/PR17.09E.html.

Chapter Four: The Predictions of Nostradamus

1. Hitchcock, *2012*, 67.
2. The Discovery Channel's documentary "Nostradamus Decoded."
3. Richard Smoley, *The Essential Nostradamus* (New York: Tarcher, 2006), 13.
4. Ibid., 23.
5. Willis and Willis, *Armageddon Now*, 299.
6. "Nostradamus Decoded."
7. Hildebrand, *2012: Is It the End?*, 105.
8. See Dan Corner, The Facts About Nostradamus and His Prophecies, at http://www.evangelicaloutreach.org/nostradamus.htm.
9. Hitchcock, *2012*, 77 (also see these passages: Deuteronomy 18:20–22; Isaiah 47:10–14; Jeremiah 27:9–10; and Revelation 21:8).
10. Smoley, *The Essential Nostradamus*, 63.
11. Ibid., 33.
12. Michael Rathford, *The Nostradamus Code: World War III* (n.p.: Truth Revealed Publishing, 2008), 3.
13. Some believe that Catherine de Medici received a copy of Nostradamus's prophecy about the death of her husband before it occurred. After King Henry II's death, she called Nostradamus to attend her in court and rewarded him for his skills.
14. Smoley, *The Essential Nostradamus*, 91.
15. The Nazi Party used this interpretation of Nostradamus's quatrains to exalt Hitler.
16. Richard Smoley cited two examples of the interpretation of this quatrain to mean an attack on New York City with extensive damage from flames, prior to 2001 (one in 1973 and the other in 1997), *The Essential Nostradamus*, 177.
17. "Nostradamus Decoded."
18. Smoley, *The Essential Nostradamus*, 187.
19. "Nostradamus Decoded."
20. Ibid.

21. Smoley, *The Essential Nostradamus*, 35.
22. Andrews and Andrews, *The Complete Idiot's Guide to 2012*, 171.
23. "Nostradamus Decoded."
24. Smoley, *The Essential Nostradamus*, 49–50.
25. It is significant to note that Dr. Osvaldo Avallone, director of the National Library, has had the drawings tested scientifically, and they have been dated in the 1800s.

Chapter Five: The Reversal of the Magnetic Poles

1. Nils Olsen and Miorana Mandea, "Rapidly Changing Flows in the Earth's Core" in the *Journal of Nature Geoscience* at www.nature.com/ngeo for 18 May 2008.
2. Willis and Willis, *Armageddon Now*, 324.
3. Ibid.
4. Andrews and Andrews, *The Complete Idiot's Guide to 2012*, 125.
5. Joseph, *Apocalypse 2012*, 51.
6. Ibid., 55.
7. Ibid., 56–57.
8. Hildebrand, *2012: Is It the End?*, 139–40.
9. See LaViolette *Earth Under Fire*, 384.
10. Jeremy Hsu, "Sloshing Inside Earth Changes Protective Magnetic Field," SPACE.com, August 18, 2008, www.space.com/scienceastronomy/080818-mm-earth-core.html.
11. Ibid.
12. Discovery Channel, "2012 Apocalypse."

Chapter Six: Collision with Planet X

1. "Pole Shift Date of May 27, 2003," http://www.zetatalk.com/index/psdate1.htm.
2. *The ZetaTalk Newsletter*, Issue 35, Sunday, May 30, 2009 at: www.Zetatalk.com.
3. See a thorough discussion of the alleged Planet Nibiru collision with Earth at: http://www.surviving-nibiru.com/.
4. Govert Schilling, *The Hunt for Planet X: New Worlds and the Fate of Pluto* (n.p.: Springer, 2008), 112.
5. Ibid., 108.

6. Ibid.
7. Ibid., 111.
8. Ibid., 115.
9. Ibid., 117.
10. Joseph, *Apocolypse 2012*, 160.
11. Ibid.
12. Ibid.
13. Schilling, *The Hunt for Planet* X, 117.

Chapter Seven: Earth's Alignment with the Galactic Plane

1. Jenkins, *The 2012 Story*, 138–58.
2. Andrews and Andrews, *The Complete Idiot's Guide to 2012*, 83.
3. Jenkins, *Maya Cosmogenesis 2012*, 112.
4. Andrews and Andrews, *The Complete Idiot's Guide to 2012*, 97.
5. Benedict, *The Mayan Prophecies for 2012*, 70–71.
6. Hitchcock, *2012*, 36.
7. Jenkins, *The 2012 Story*, 138–58.
8. See his Web site, www.jiroolcott.com.
9. Jiro Olcott, "2012 Earth's Polar Reversal," www.jiroolcott.com/2012.
html.
10. Joseph, *Apocalypse 2012*, 124.
11. Ibid.,131.
12. Ibid., 135.
13. http://astrobiology.nasa.gov/ask-an-astrobiologist/intro/niburu-and-doomsday-2012-questions-and-answers. (Question 11)
14. Ibid., questions 12 and 13.
   15.   Jiro Olcott, "St. Michael and Alignment," www.jiroolcott.com/
st_michael_alignment.html.

Chapter Eight: Eruption of the Super Volcano

1. Greg Breining, *Super Volcano: The Ticking Time Bomb Beneath Yellowstone National Park* (St. paul: Voyaguer, 2010), 53.
2. Ibid., 17.
3. Joseph, *Apocalypse 2012*, 60.
4. Breining, *Super Volcano*, 13.
5. Nur, *Apocalypse*, 39.

6. See "Yellowstone Lake Earthquake Swarm Summary as of 6 January 2009," at http://volcanoes.usgs.gov/yvo/publications/2009/09swarm.php.
7. Quoted in *LiveScience.com* "Super Volcano Will Challenge Civilization, Geologist Warns," March 8, 2005.
8. Breining, *Super Volcano*, 229.
9. "Super Volcano Will Challenge Civilization, Geologist Warns."
10. See Stephen Sparks's article, "Super-Eruptions Pose Global Threat '5–10 Times More Likely Than Asteroid Impact,'" at www.innovations-report.com.
11. Discovery Channel, "2012 Apocalypse."
12. Breining, *Super Volcano*, 21.
13. Joseph, *Apocalypse 2012*, 61.
14. Breining, *Super Volcano*, 17–19.
15. Ibid., 236.
16. Ibid., 235.
17. Andrews and Andrews, *The Complete Idiot's Guide to 2012*, 128.
18. Breining, *Super Volcano*, 21.
19. Ibid.
20. Ibid., 18.

Chapter Nine: The Web Bot Project

1. Andrews and Andrews, *The Complete Idiot's Guide to 2012*, 161.
2. Tom Chivers, "'Web-bot project' makes prophecy of 2012 apocalypse," Telegraph.co.uk, September 24, 2009.
3. Hildebrand, *2012: Is It the End?*, 223–24.
4. Ben Tremblay, "Web Bot—What Is It?" at www.dailycommonsense.com.
5. Hitchcock, *2012*, 98.

Chapter Ten: Religiuos Predictions of the End of the World

1. Terence McKenna, "Approaching Timewave Zero," at www.drugnerd.com.
2. Hildebrand, *2012: Is It the End?*, 52.
3. McKenna, "Approaching Timewave Zero."
4. Ibid.

5. Ibid.

6. Ibid.

7. Terence McKenna, *True Hallucinations: Being an Account of the Author's Extraordinary Experiences in the Devil's Paradise* (San Francisco: HarperOne, 1994), 1–2.

8. Ibid., quoted in a book review by Jordan S. Gruber at Enlightenment.com.

9. Ibid.

10. McKenna, "Approaching the Timewave Zero."

11. Ibid.

12. Willis and Willis, *Armageddon Now*, 93.

13. McKenna, *True Hallucinations*, 1.

14. McKenna, "Approaching the Timewave Zero."

15. Ibid.

16. Ibid.

17. Joseph, *Apocalypse 2012*.

18. Hildebrand, *2012: Is It the End?*, 57.

19. Abu-Shabanah, Abdel Khalek Himmat (translator), *Al Montakhab: Interpretation of the Holy Quran – Arabic/English*.

20. Hildebrand, *2012*, 213.

21. Michael Baigent, *Racing Toward Armageddon: The Three Great Religions and the Plot to End the World* (New York: HarperCollins, 2009), 186.

22. Ibid., 193–205.

23. Hildebrand, *2012*, 213.

24. Ibid., 205.

25. Ibid., 165.

26. Ibid., 169–170.

27. Willis and Willis, *Armageddon Now*, 229.

28. Ibid., 231.

29. "A Message from Chief Dan Evehema," www.ilhawaii.net/~story/chiefdan.html.

30. "Hopi Indians," www.apocalypse-soon.com/prophecies_of_hopi_indians.htm.

31. Hildebrand, *2012: Is It the End?*, 72.

32. Ibid., 72.

33. "Hopi Prophecy Fulfilled," Wolflodge.org, www.wolflodge.org/bluestar/bluestar.htm.

34. Willis and Willis, *Armageddon Now*, 244.

35. Hildebrand, *2012: Is It the End?*, 79.

36. David Jeremiah, *Until Christ Returns* (Nashville: Thomas Nelson, 2007), 3.

37. Harold Camping, "We Are Almost There" on FamilyRadio.com.

38. Ibid.

39. Jeremiah, *Until Christ Returns*, 70–73.

40. Ibid., 84–85.

Chapter Twelve: Preparation fo rthe End of the World

1. See ExtremeSurvival.net.

2. Hildebrand, *2012*, 249.

Epilogue for Christians

1. Jeremiah, *Until Christ Returns*, 77–78.

MAJOR WORKS CITED

Andrews, Synthia and Colin Andrews. *The Complete Idiot's Guide to 2012*. New York: Penguin, 2008.

Argüelles, José. *The Mayan Factor: Path Beyond Technology*. Rochester, VT: Bear and Company, 1996.

Baigent, Michael. *Racing Toward Armageddon: The Three Great Religions and the Plot to End the World*. New York: HarperCollins, 2009.

Benedict, Gerald. *The Mayan Prophecies for 2012*. London: Watkins Publishing, 2009.

Breining, Greg. *Super Volcano: The Ticking Time Bomb Beneath Yellowstone National Park*. St. Paul, MN: Voyageur Press, 2007.

Browne, Sylvia. *End of Days: Predictions and Prophecies About the End of the World*. New York: Penguin, 2008.

Christenson, Allen J. *Popul Vuh: The Sacred Book of the Maya*. New York: O Books, 2003.

Coe, Michael D. *The Maya*. Great Britain: Thames and Hudson, 1966.

Drosnin, Michael. *Bible Code II: The Countdown*. New York: Viking/Penguin, 2002.

Drosnin, Michael. *The Bible Code*. New York: Touchstone and Simon & Schuster, 1997.

Geryl, Patrick and Gino Ratinckx. *The Orion Prophecy: Will the World Be Destroyed in 2012?* Kempton, IL: Adventures Unlimited Press, 2001.

Hildebrand, Lloyd B. *2012: Is This the End?* Alachua, FL: Bridge Logos, 2009.

Himmat, Abu-Shabanah, Abdel Khalek (translator). *Al Montakhab: The Interpretation of the Holy Quran—Arabic/ English*. Cairo: Supreme Council for Islamic Affairs, 1993.

Hitchcock, Mark. *2012, The Bible, and the End of the World* (Eugene, OR: Harvest House, 2009).

Jenkins, John Major. *Maya Cosmogenesis 2012: The True Meaning of the Maya Calendar End-Date*. Rochester, VT: Bear and Company, 1998.

———. *The 2012 Story: The Myths, Fallacies, and Truth Behind the Most Intriguing Date in History*. New York: Penguin, 2009.

Jeremiah, David. *Until Christ Returns: Living Faithfully Today While We Wait for Our Glorious Tomorrow*. Nashville: Thomas Nelson, 1999.

Joseph, Lawrence E. *Apocalypse 2012: A Scientific Investigation into Civilization's End*. New York: Morgan Road Books, 2007.

LaViolette, Paul A. *Earth Under Fire: Humanity's Survival of the Ice Age*. Rochester, Vermont: Bear and Company, 2005.

McKenna, Terence. *True Hallucinations: Being an Account of the Author's Extraordinary Experiences in the Devil's Paradise*. New York: HarperCollins, 1994.

McKenna, Terence and Dennis McKenna. *The Invisible Landscape: Mind, Hallucinogens, and the I Ching*. San Francisco: HarperSanFrancisco, 1993.

Nur, Amos. *Apocalypse: Earthquakes, Archaeology, and the Wrath of God*. Princeton: Princeton University Press, 2008.

———. *Apocalypse: Earthquakes, Archaeology, and the Wrath of God*. Princeton/Oxford: Princeton University Press, 2008.

Payne, J. Barton. *Encyclopedia of Biblical Prophecy: The Complete Guide to Scriptural Predictions and Their Fulfillment.* New York: Harper and Row, 1973.

Petersen, John L. *A Vision for 2012: Planning for Extraordinary Change.* Golden, CO: Fulcrum, 2008.

Rathford, Michael. *The Nostradamus Code: World War III.* Kearney, NE: Morris Publishing, 2008.

Schele, Linda and David Freidel. *A Forest of Kings: The Untold Story of the Ancient Maya.* New York: William Morrow and Company, 1990.

Schilling, Govert. *The Hunt for Planet X: New Worlds and the Fate of Pluto.* New York: Copernicus Books, 2009.

Smith, Stephanie and Daniel Pinchbeck. *2012: Biography of a Time Traveler: The Journey of José Argüelles.* Franklin Lanes, NJ: Career Press, 2009.

Smoley, Richard. *The Essential Nostradamus.* New York: Penguin, 2006.

Willis, Jim and Barbara Willis. *Armageddon Now: The End of the World A to Z.* Detroit: Visible Ink Press, 2006.

Witztum, Doron, Eliyahu Rips and Yoav Rosenberg. "Equidistant Letter Sequences in the Book of Genesis." *Statistical Science* 9, no. 3 (1994): 429–38.

ACKNOWLEDGMENTS

I WOULD LIKE TO EXPRESS MY GRATITUDE TO MR. FRED Evans Jr. and Mr. Rick Shear of the Thomas Nelson Publishing Company, who first suggested this project to me and have given me continual support and help as the writing of it progressed.

ABOUT THE AUTHOR

RAYMOND C. HUNDLEY, PHD HAS BEEN A YOUTH worker, pastor, missionary, seminary professor, Cambridge scholar, university professor, author, and international conference speaker. He received his Master of Arts in Religion in hermeneutics from Asbury Theological Seminary, a Master of Letters in theology from the University of Cambridge, and a PhD in systematic theology from Trinity Evangelical Divinity School. He lives in Sarasota, FL with his wife.

STUDY GUIDE FOR INDIVIDUALS OR GROUPS

Introduction:

1. What is our "prediction addiction," and to what extent do you share that interest?

2. What method does Michael Drosnin use in his book *Bible Code*, and what does he predict for 2012 on that basis?

3. What is José Argüelles's concept of "harmonic convergence," and how does it inform his view of 2012?

4. How similar or different is your reaction to the 2012 reports from the reaction of the young person who wrote to the 2012 Web site?

5. What is the purpose of Sony's bogus "Institute for Human Continuity"—both their expressed purpose and their real purpose?

6. If you have seen the movie *2012*, how did you feel when the movie was over? (If you haven't seen it, what is your response to the summary of the film given here?)

7. What are the ten basic 2012 arguments that will be covered in this book?

8. What may well be the most constructive result of the 2012 phenomenon?

Chapter One: The Mayan Factor

1. What was the extension of the Mayan Empire during its Classic Period?

2. Why did the Maya use blood sacrifices in their rituals?

3. How did those rituals cause the Maya to become expert astronomers?

4. On what dates did the Mayan calendar begin and end?

5. Which Mayan experts identify 2012 as the end of the world, and which see it as a transition to a new age for the planet? Why?

6. Even if it could be established that the Maya saw 2012 as the end of the world, what else would have to be proved about them to accept that date as valid?

7. What is your overall impression of the significance of the end of the Mayan calendar on December 21, 2012?

Chapter Two: Solar Storms

1. What is the relevance of the 1859 solar storm to the 2012 debate?

2. What are NASA and NCAR scientists predicting about solar storms in the future?

3. What are coronal mass ejections, and how could they affect Earth?

4. According to Ken Tegnell of the NOAA, what could a severe solar storm do to the world?

5. What is your overall impression of the contribution of solar storm predictions to 2012 possibilities?

Chapter Three: CERN and the Large Hadron Collider

1. What is CERN, and what is its mandate?

2. What was the Large Hadron Collider built to do? How does it work?

3. What do the CERN scientists hope to simulate, and why is that important?

4. What are some of the potential risks of using the Large Hadron Collider?

5. What happened in 2008 that made many people fear the safety measures of the collider?

6. What have the scientists at CERN done in response to those concerns, and what was its result?

7. What have prominent scientists said about the dangers at CERN?

8. What is your overall impression of the risks involved in firing up the Large Hadron Collider?

Chapter Four: The Predictions of Nostradamus

1. Who was Nostradamus, and when did he live?

2. What was Nostradamus's most famous work, and when was it published?

3. Describe five of Nostradamus's most celebrated predictions.

4. What is the *Lost Book of Nostradamus*, and what does it contain?

5. Name the seven drawings that Nostradamus experts believe predict the events leading up to the end of the world.

6. Do you agree with the interpretations of the drawings given by Bridges and Baines?

7. What is your overall impression of the weight of these predictions for a future 2012 doomsday event?

Chapter Five: The Reversal of the Magnetic Poles

1. Define "geomagnetic reversal."

2. What is the "South Atlantic Anomaly"?

3. What events does John Rennie of *Scientific American* foresee if there is a reversal of the magnetic poles?

4. What is the connection between the magnetic pole reversal and the solar storms predicted by NASA scientists for 2012?

5. What is your overall assessment of the probability that this reversal will be destructive and occur in 2012?

Chapter Six: Collision with Planet X

1. Who began the Planet X predictions, and what was the source of her information?

2. What do the Zetas supposedly predict that the near collision with Planet X will do to Earth?

3. What does Lieder allege that the establishment is doing to divert attention from her revelations about Planet X? Why would they do that?

4. What is the other name for Planet X?

5. What is Dr. David Morrison's (NAI senior scientist) view of Planet X?

6. How would you judge the likelihood that this collision will take place?

Chapter Seven: Earth's Alignment with the Galactic Plane

1. Who has been the main proponent of the galactic alignment theory?

2. What are the "galactic center" and the "galactic equator"?

3. Does Jenkins believe the solar system will pass through the center of the Milky Way Galaxy?

4. What does Jenkins believe will happen in 2012 as a result of galactic alignment?

5. On the other hand, what does Jiro Olcott believe will happen in 2012 as a result of galactic alignment?

6. What is Dr. David Morrison's view about the galactic alignment and galactic intersection predictions?

7. According to Morrison, how far is the solar system from the center of the galaxy?

8. What is your overall impression of the seriousness of this argument?

Chapter Eight: Eruption of the Super Volcano

1. Where is the world's largest volcano found?
2. What have the Yellowstone geologists noticed about the Yellowstone cauldron, and what could that mean?
3. What is an "earthquake swarm," and how does it relate to Yellowstone?
4. What did Stephen Self and his colleagues report to the British Natural Hazard Working Group about the results of super volcano eruptions?
5. What is Stephen Sparks's prediction about super eruptions?
6. What could the eruption of underwater super volcanoes cause?
7. What effect would a Yellowstone volcanic eruption have on the United States?
8. What have Al-Qaeda terrorists threatened to do, and what would be the result?
9. What is your overall evaluation of the threat of a super volcano eruption?

Chapter Nine: The Web Bot Project

1. What is the Web Bot Project, and how does it work?

2. What events have the Web Bot Project accurately predicted, according to Clif High?

3. What has the Web Bot Project predicted for 2012?

4. What are the two criticisms of the project by its detractors?

5. What is your impression of the accuracy of the Web Bot Project's 2012 predictions?

Chapter Ten: Religious Predictions of the End of the World
I Ching and Timewave Zero

1. What is the Timewave Zero method for interpreting the I Ching?

2. According to the McKennas' method, what will happen on December 21, 2012?

3. Why did the McKennas use natural psychedelic drugs?

4. How does that use of drugs affect the credibility of their conclusions? Why?

Islamic Prophecies

1. Did Muhammad predict a definite date for the end of the world?

2. How did Muhammad describe the end of the world?

3. What do some modern Islamic terrorists believe must precede the end of the world and the coming of the Muslim messiah (the Mahdi)?

Hindu Teachings

1. How does the Hindu religion predict the end of the world?
2. What is the "Night of Brahman" in Hindu theology?
3. Does the Hindu view predict an end of the world?

Hopi Religion

1. How do the elders of the Hopi nation describe the "Great Day of Purification"?
2. How do the Hopi believe the end of the world can be avoided?
3. What did a Hopi spiritual leader predict about the year 2007?

Our Lady of Emmitsburg

1. What are the four basic elements of the message from the Virgin Mary to Gianna Sullivan?
2. What does this message share with other 2012 predictions?
3. How did the Archdiocese of Baltimore react to this message?

Prophecies in Hebrew Scriptures

1. What term did the Hebrew prophets use to name the end of the world?

2. Name five key elements of the Hebrew prophets' descriptions of the end of the world.

Prophecies in the New Testament

1. Name seven descriptions of the end of the world in the New Testament.
2. What did Jesus tell His disciples about setting a date for His Second Coming and the end of the world?
3. What did Jack Van Impe use to establish his date of December 21, 2012, for the end of the world, and how do Van Impe and Harold Camping try to get around Jesus' teaching that no one knows when the end will come?
4. What chapter in the New Testament reveals the most about the Day of the Lord?

Overview

1. How have these religious predictions added to the 2012 doomsday theories?

Chapter Eleven: Final Evaluations

1. How did the hypothetical description of December 21, 2012, affect you personally?
2. Rate each of the ten arguments for a 2012 doomsday by whether it is very convincing, somewhat convincing, not very convincing, or not at all convincing.

3. In summary, how convinced are you that the world will end in 2012?

Chapter Twelve: Preparation for the End of the World

1. What do you think about the effectiveness of building underground bunkers to survive the possible cataclysm of 2012?

2. Describe the way millions of Christians have faced their own personal "end of the world" in death.

3. What is the best antidote to the fear and dread that 2012 predictions can cause?

4. What does each of the three steps—believe, admit, ask—toward a personal relationship with Jesus Christ mean?

5. What did Jesus promise His followers in John 14?

6. Do you have a personal relationship with Jesus Christ? Has He forgiven your sins and accepted you as His son or daughter, giving you eternal life? If not, would you like to ask Him to right now?

Epilogue for Christians

1. What does Peter say is the best preparation for the end of the world? Can we do that in our own strength?

2. What do we need to be asking ourselves constantly in the light of Jesus' return?

3. What is the best way to be ready to greet the Lord with joy when He returns?

4. What would change in your life if you really believed the world was going to end on December 21, 2012?

5. What kind of final testimony would you be able to give if your death came today?

6. In the ending prayer of this book, what three things is the Lord asked to give us—grace to meet death with _____, _____, and _____?

7. How has the study of this book touched your life?